The Evolution of the Con

1926-1972

STUDENTS LIBRARY OF EDUCATION

The Evolution of the Comprehensive School, 1926-1972

David Rubinstein
Lecturer in Social History, University of Hull

and

Brian Simon
Professor of Education, University of Leicester

ROUTLEDGE & KEGAN PAUL
LONDON

First published in 1969
as The *Evolution of the Comprehensive School, 1926-1966*
by Routledge & Kegan Paul Ltd
Broadway House, 68-74 Carter Lane,
London EC4V 5EL
Second edition 1973

Printed in Great Britain by
Unwin Brothers Limited
The Gresham Press
Old Woking, Surrey
© *David Rubinstein and Brian Simon 1969, 1973*

ISBN 0 7100 7654 1 (C)
ISBN 0 7100 7655 X (P)

Acknowledgements

Acknowledgements are made to Her Majesty's Stationery Office and the Registrar General for permission to reprint copyright material.

THE STUDENTS LIBRARY OF EDUCATION has been designed to meet the needs of students of Education at Colleges of Education and at University Institutes and Departments. It will also be valuable for practising teachers and educationists. The series takes full account of the latest developments in teacher-training and of new methods and approaches in education. Separate volumes will provide authoritative and up-to-date accounts of the topics within the major fields of sociology, philosophy and history of education, educational psychology, and method. Care has been taken that specialist topics are treated lucidly and usefully for the nonspecialist reader. Altogether, the Students' Library of Education will provide a comprehensive introduction and guide to anyone concerned with the study of education, and with educational theory and practice.

J. W. TIBBLE

The Evolution of the Comprehensive School, 1926-72, in the history section of the series, is intended to follow Gerald Bernbaum's *Social Change and the Schools, 1918-44*. Unlike the latter book, however, it does not attempt to deal with all aspects of educational change during the period it covers. The focus is deliberately on one aspect— secondary education, and within that on the origin and development of the common, or comprehensive school.

While the book is, therefore, mainly concerned with the period following the Second World War, and the Education Act of 1944, some attention is necessarily devoted to the 1920s and '30s, when the foundations for the tripartite system of secondary education were laid, but when teachers and others were already proposing the establishment of what was then known as the 'multilateral' school. The movement for comprehensive education is then traced, and the experiences of the early schools of a new type discussed. The book ends with an analysis of Circular 10/65 (July 1965), which marked the decision to develop various types of comprehensive schools as national policy.

Many students will go on to teach in comprehensive schools now and in the future. This book aims to familiarise these and others with the historical background of this movement, and with the main reasons for the decision to establish a national system of comprehensive education.

The second edition of this book includes a new chapter which covers the period from 1966 to 1972, including the withdrawal of Circular 10/65 by the Conservative government elected in the summer of 1970, and events since that time.

B. SIMON

Contents

CONTENTS

Preface

In July, 1965, the Secretary of State for Education and Science in a Labour government issued the now famous Circular 10/65 to local education authorities asking them to submit plans for the reorganisation of secondary schools on comprehensive lines. This opened the way for a re-orientation of secondary education. There had been significant moves in this direction over many years accompanied by considerable political controversy. But in June 1967 the leader of the opposition made a statement which implied general acceptance of the comprehensive pattern, whatever differences might remain on particular points. The place of the 'public' schools, and those that receive a 'direct grant' from the Department of Education are matters which, in 1968, still await decision. But secondary schools providing for the great majority of children which, since 1944, have been organised mainly in the form of selective grammar schools for the few and modern schools for the many, are being transformed to eliminate selection at an early age.

To grasp the significance of this change of direction, and to trace the first steps towards the single secondary school, it is necessary first to look briefly at the structure of the educational system before 1944. Two volumes in the history section of the Students' Library of Education have already dealt with this period from different angles—Eric

Eaglesham's study of the 1902 Act *The Foundations of Twentieth Century Education in England* (1967) and Gerald Bernbaum's *Social Change and the Schools, 1918-1944* (1967). Here attention will be confined to aspects of organisation and practice which bear directly on the question at issue—that is, whether the secondary system should consist of different types of school, or whether it should be unified. Policies and attitudes have fluctuated over the years as a result of psychological research, sociological analysis, and developments within the schools themselves in the light of wider economic, social and political change. But some local authorities have favoured comprehensive schools since 1944, and these have gradually increased in number and influence.

Even in 1968, however, there remain some areas where there is little direct knowledge of comprehensive schools and of the educational ends pursued. Teachers in training cannot always practice in such schools, nor easily visit them. While, in so short a study, not a great deal can be said about the strictly educational aspects of the comprehensive school, the question will be touched on in the course of outlining the history of its development. The subject has not yet been incorporated in the history of twentieth-century education, but this sketch may help to throw into relief the new tasks that await a new generation of teachers entering the schools. One of the authors has had inside experience, having been educated in comprehensive schools in the United States and taught in three comprehensive schools in London; the other has studied developments over the past quarter of a century, more recently in connection with the education of intending teachers.

1

The background of the comprehensive school

Elementary and secondary schools: two parallel systems

It is well known that the Education Act of 1902 laid the basis for a national system of secondary education, but it is not so often understood how limited a system this at first was, however great the improvement on what had gone before. Nor is it always realised that secondary schools were not 'end-on' to the elementary schools which provided for the vast majority of children, but formed a parallel system.

The typical elementary school in the early years of this century was an all-age school, recruiting pupils at the age of five or earlier, and keeping them until they reached the statutory school leaving age—which was only generally raised to fourteen in 1921. In these schools education was free, but a considerable number of children ceased attending full-time at the age of twelve when they were permitted to go to work half-time. While financial pressures caused many parents to put children to work as early as possible—free schooling did not make up for loss of earnings—there were also demands from industry for 'little fingers' at the machines. As late as 1936, one of the chief arguments against raising the school leaving age was that the children were needed in the factories, and it was not until 1947 that the leaving age was in fact raised to fifteen, ✗

a measure for which reformers had been pressing for thirty years or more. Elementary education, though its scope was gradually extended, was therefore still seen as a type of education designed for the children of the working class.

By contrast the system of secondary schools, consolidated after 1902, was frankly intended for a minority. Whether endowed grammar schools, which now received grants of public money, or the new schools established and fully maintained by local authorities, these schools were linked with the universities, both ancient and modern, rather than with the elementary schools. Recruiting children at seven or eight and keeping them until fifteen or over, charging fees, they provided a parallel system of education which was only tenuously connected with the basic elementary system until 1907. At that date a link was established between the two systems when the Liberal government, returned the previous year, laid down as a condition of making grants of public money that twenty-five per cent of places must be set aside as 'free places' for entrants from the 'public elementary schools'. From this provision, supplementing the scholarship system already existing and gradually extending in scope, stemmed what was then known as 'the scholarship', later as 'the eleven plus'.

The new secondary system was established at the expense of the 'higher grade schools' run by the larger School Boards, which tended to emphasise science and technology and had provided a natural 'end-on' extension of elementary education into the secondary range. (The School Boards, set up in 1870, were themselves superseded as education authorities in 1902 by counties, county boroughs and some urban districts with more limited powers.) Only some of these schools survived as 'higher elementary' schools within the elementary system, others were assimilated into the secondary system and shaped

2

on academic lines. From 1902 an increasingly sharp division was made between 'technical' and 'secondary' education, which came under different departments of the Board of Education, and it was the clear aim of official policy, imposed by inspection and other means, to shape secondary schools on the pattern of the larger endowed grammar schools and the 'public' schools. This aim was generally realised, so that to pass from elementary to secondary school was to pass from one world into another. It was seen as a main task of the secondary school to 'assimilate' ex-elementary pupils to a new sphere of life, not only in terms of an academic curriculum but also in the kind of 'total' environment designed to form character and outlook, for which public schools were known.

A clear differentiation between types of school was, then, built into the national system of education as it developed to cover the secondary stage. This was to influence all subsequent thinking on the question of secondary education for all, a demand that began to be clearly advanced after the first world war. For instance, those who wished to see the schooling of the majority extended did not necessarily consider it desirable for all to go to a secondary school of the existing type, with an academic curriculum largely dictated by university requirements. Different forms of secondary education, on the lines that had begun fruitfully to develop in higher grade schools before 1902, seemed more desirable, both from the point of view of social needs and the welfare of the children. On the other hand some saw the dangers of further differentiation and called for a unified secondary school incorporating a variety of forms of education—this later became known as the 'multilateral' or 'many-sided' school.

After 1918 these views gradually took shape, and it is to the 1920s that the origin of ideas which have since developed in the movement to establish comprehensive

3

schools can be traced. But there was a much stronger body of opinion in favour of differentiation. A brief outline may be given of these two trends, for the history of our subject during the inter-war years can be seen, in part, in terms of a tension between them. We may begin, however, by looking further back.

Trends up to 1914

'Notwithstanding the great gulf that separates the middle from the working classes, and the middle from the higher classes in this country,' said Richard Cobden, the anti-Corn Law leader, in 1854, 'nothing would tend so much to break down that barrier as to erect common schools of so superior a quality that people should find nowhere in their vicinity an opportunity—whatever the class might be—of giving the children a better opportunity than by availing themselves of the facilities afforded by the common schools.' This was a radical viewpoint, advanced at a time when the reconstruction of the country's educational system was first coming under serious consideration. Influenced in part by acquaintance with the newly reorganised school system of Massachusetts, it also derived from what had been a traditional way of providing schools in England; many grammar schools founded in the sixteenth and seventeenth centuries were intended to provide a free education for the children in the locality. But the policy eventually adopted leant in an opposite direction, that of establishing grades of school for the various social classes, differentiated both by curriculum and by leaving age. This policy, clearly outlined in these terms by the Schools Inquiry Commission in 1868, was carried out in the last three decades of the nineteenth century.

There had been earlier calls for a unified system of education by those who spoke for the working class. In

4

1841 the Chartist leader, William Lovett, published a plan for educational advance based on the principle of the common school. Later, in the 1880s, when new Board Schools were throwing up 'higher tops' and some flourishing 'higher grade' schools had developed, Thomas Smyth, described as 'a representative of the working class', put a similar view to a Royal Commission appointed to consider the development of elementary education. Elementary schools, he said, should give a general, not a vocational education; in particular, separate schools for different social classes should be superseded by a single school 'common to all', as the best means of raising the general level of education.

This standpoint was reiterated in a memorial presented in 1894 to the Bryce Commission (inquiring into secondary education) 'on behalf of Trades and Labour Councils [and] Co-operative Societies'. Criticising the parallel system of elementary and so-called secondary schools it pointed out (as was the case) that the latter provided a primary education for the 'wealthier section of the community'. It affirmed that 'the distinction of primary and secondary schools should be . . . strictly and solely *educational*, marking the successive stages of an educational curriculum; and not *social*, marking merely different grades of social rank'. All children should be educated together in a common school 'and thus realise and enjoy in their youth common interests and pursuits as the children of one country' (Simon, 1965, 126, 200-1).

The implementing of the 1902 Act, which ended the upward growth of the elementary school and erected new barriers between technical and secondary education, created a new situation. At this time there were conscious efforts to prevent the new secondary system developing as an exclusively 'class' system by opening it up to some degree to the working class. But to make a quarter of the places freely available to entrants from elementary schools did not achieve this. The 'secondary' system remained a parallel system with a quite different approach and outlook from that of the elementary schools. Only a small proportion of elementary school children could enter through the filter of the 'scholarship' examination which became increasingly competitive. The other pupils were fee-payers some of whom entered preparatory departments at the age of seven or eight and then simply passed up the school. The relics of this pattern may still be found in some 'direct grant' schools which still run their own preparatory departments.

If this was the major divide in the educational system, there were other differentiated schools within the elementary system deriving from past history and present needs. The School Boards, responsible for all the children in their areas not otherwise provided for, had grappled with the task of establishing special facilities for the handicapped and delinquent, for trade training at various levels, and for higher grade teaching in special departments or schools. After the 1902 Act these schools continued under the new authorities, to be supplemented in the larger towns by additional 'central' and junior technical schools, the former having a selective entry and giving a longer course than the normal schools could provide. It was in this situation that some began to argue that differentiation of schools was necessary and desirable and should be the pattern of future development.

'What we have learned, gradually and slowly,' wrote Sidney Webb, who was closely involved in the development of London's educational system between 1890 and 1910, 'is that nothing worthy of the name of a national system of education can be built up out of schools of a single undifferentiated type, however numerous and however excellent they may be.' While the educational re-

6

formers of the mid-nineteenth century were right 'to insist on the provision of schools by wholesale', now that practically all children were in school the time was ripe for a further advance. What was needed in all populous centres was 'the progressive differentiation of the publicly provided school—the "common school" of our Radical grandfathers [i.e. Cobden]—into a number of specialised schools each more accurately fitting the needs of a particular section of children'. Already London had provided, in addition to the normal boys', girls' and infants' schools, 'three or four different types of higher elementary schools', schools for the blind and deaf, 'open air' and 'ringworm' schools, truant and industrial schools, domestic economy schools, 'a dozen varieties of "trade school"; and, among all the other specialisations, not only one but three or four different types of secondary school' (Webb, 1908, 288-9).

This quotation is given at some length as an example of thinking which derived largely from the existing situation, in this case in what was by far the greatest urban centre in the country. Few other areas, however, were large enough to develop different types of school on this scale—and even in London the great majority of children remained in 'all-age' elementary schools. The principle of differentiation, as outlined by Webb, however, was already well established before the first world war, its main purpose being to fit individual children—other than those who went straight to work on leaving the elementary school— for specific industrial or commercial employment. The period between the wars was to see this process carried a great deal further.

'Selection by differentiation'—the Hadow reports

The keynote of the inter-war period was the deliberate

development of different types of post-primary schools (for children over the age of eleven) and, together with this, of methods of differentiating between children *within* each type of school, the process known as 'streaming'. Both processes were closely related to each other from a practical and theoretical point of view.

The Education Act of 1918 provided for the raising of the school leaving age to fourteen, and this was brought into effect in 1921, the aim being to raise it further to fifteen as soon as possible. This meant the end of half-time exemptions and brought the whole thirteen-fourteen age group into full-time education. At the same time there was a growing pressure on the secondary schools which had insufficient accommodation even for all those children who qualified for a place, while the Labour movement was campaigning for 'secondary education for all'.

It was now becoming clear that some reorganisation of education for children over the age of eleven was urgent. The all-age elementary school, often with only one class for each year-group, could not cope effectively with the older children, particularly in the provision of courses to meet their needs. The Consultative Committee to the Board of Education was therefore asked to report on 'the organisation, objective and curriculum' of courses of study suitable for children who will remain at school until fifteen.

The secondary (grammar) schools were, however, deliberately excluded from the Committee's terms of reference; it was clearly the policy of the Board of Education that these schools should remain separate. The Committee agreed with this policy. In its report *The Education of the Adolescent* (1926) it proposed that elementary schools should be divided into primary schools on the one hand, and post-primary schools on the other, the age of transfer being about eleven. While there should be a single primary

8

school, however, post-primary schools should consist of a variety of types. In addition to the secondary schools (following 'a predominantly literary or scientific curriculum') there should be central schools (giving a four year course 'with a realistic or practical trend'), non-selective central or 'modern' schools, as the committee proposed they should be called (for the bulk of the pupils), 'senior classes' for those for whom it was impossible to provide a separate school, and, finally, junior technical and trade schools. In effect, the Hadow Committee (as it came to be called after its chairman) proposed that there should be five different types of post-primary school parallel to the existing secondary schools.

These five types were, in fact, all in existence in various parts of the country when the Hadow Committee reported, although at that time containing only about 5 per cent of elementary school children aged eleven to fourteen. The report reinforced existing developments which had taken place in response to social trends and political pressures. Its main importance lay in its recommendation for the break at eleven. By this age, the Committee argued, children have given 'some indication of difference in interest and abilities sufficient to make it possible and desirable to cater for them by means of schools of varying types but which have, nevertheless, a broad common foundation'. Consequently a new phase of education should commence for all at eleven. 'We regard the general recognition that the aim of educational policy must be, not merely to select a minority of children for the second stage, but to secure that the second stage is sufficiently elastic, and contains schools of sufficient variety of type, to meet the needs of all children, as one of the most notable advances,' runs the report. 'Thus all go forward, though along different paths. Selection by differentiation takes the place of selection by elimination' (Hadow, 1926, 74, 78).

This was to blur over the fact that selection for 'secondary' education—that is, for the full secondary (now grammar) schools—would inevitably continue to be selection by elimination of the majority, so long as the demand for secondary education greatly exceeded the supply of places. In spite of the Hadow Committee's recommendation that all post-primary education should be regarded as secondary in character, the new 'senior' or 'modern' schools remained squarely classified as elementary, controlled by the elementary code of regulations rather than the secondary. Though the new buildings were greatly superior to those of the all-age elementary schools, they were inferior to those provided for the full secondary school, while the salaries of teachers, grants for equipment, and so on were calculated on a scale that was a great deal less generous.

It is important to note that the Hadow phrase 'selection by differentiation' covered a more far-reaching conception of differentiating children than there had previously been, and from a much earlier age. As the primary and post-primary schools were separated out, children were to be increasingly graded and classified within them. It was later officially stated that the Hadow principle of reorganisation resulted from 'recognition of the difficulties of classification in schools organised on traditional lines'. Once junior and senior schools were separated, and each sufficiently large in size, it became possible to arrange promotion by age 'and classification by ability at the same time'. This was the best means of meeting the needs of 'different types of child' for it enabled the provision of complete courses of work 'of a differentiated kind' which could be followed uninterruptedly 'by each type of child' throughout his school life (*Handbook of Suggestions for Teachers*, 1937 ed., 33-4).

In fact, attention concentrated after 1926 on providing

10

senior, and junior, schools large enough to accommodate three or four parallel classes in each year group. By the late 1920s, then, official policy favoured not only a differentiation of post-primary schools but also the classification of children within schools (including primary schools) into parallel 'streams' following different courses with different objectives.

This was to go much further than before in emphasising the different needs of different 'types' of child. In fact what was essentially a system of organising the product of various stages of historical development, had become transmuted into a set of educational principles, to be applied not only in shaping the system of schools but also the internal organisation of each school. How had this come about?

The theory of intelligence and selective tests

In the post-war period there was a growing interest in diagnosing qualities of mind which, so far as the educational system was concerned, derived primarily from the need to select children at eleven for secondary schools. There was, in addition, increasing criticism of the Junior Scholarship Examination itself; it was argued that this was not selecting those most capable of benefiting from a secondary education. There was also concern that children from poor homes were often at a grave disadvantage in a competitive examination. If some form of relatively 'culture-free' test could be devised, to measure intellectual 'capacity', as apart from attainment, this would be fairer to the children and would relieve the pressure on schools now forced to prepare children for the examination.

That it was thought possible to construct tests of this kind was the result of developments in psychological research of a particular kind, deriving mainly from the work of Francis Galton. It is enough to say here, since there is no space to go into details, that psychologists were becoming increasingly interested in the measurement of mental abilities and many were convinced that these abilities were inherited. While attention was at first given to various abilities, in time it was concentrated on isolating and measuring what came to be regarded as the dominant mental power, 'intelligence'. There developed a whole school of psychologists, or 'psychometrists' as they were often called; among the leading members in this country in the early 1920s were Charles Spearman, Godfrey Thomson and Cyril (now Sir Cyril) Burt. Although opinions differed on various points, most were generally agreed on the main premiss, that 'intelligence' is an innate quality of mind and the determining factor in mental development. As Cyril Burt was to write in 1934, summarising the conclusions reached:

By intelligence the psychologist understands inborn, all-round intellectual ability. It is inherited, or at least innate, not due to teaching or training; it is intellectual, not emotional or moral, and remains uninfluenced by industry or zeal; it is general, not specific, i.e. it is not limited to any particular kind of work, but enters into all we do or say or think. Of all our mental qualities, it is the most far-reaching; fortunately it can be measured with accuracy and ease (Burt, 1934, 28-9).

The crucial aspect of this theory, so far as educational provision and methods were concerned, was the belief that every child is born with a given quota of 'intelligence' which remains constant throughout his life—that this key quality is fixed and unchangeable, a direct product of genetic endowment and not subject to any educational influence. If this key quality could, as was said, be accurately measured by a test then the educational administrator was provided with a tool which could be used not only in selecting the most intelligent pupils for a full secondary education, but also in planning other forms.

The Consultative Committee had already issued a report on *Tests of Educable Capacity* in 1924. In its 1926 report it noted that it was the arguments of psychologists which had been decisive in producing the recommendation that there be different types of post-primary school. Indeed, it was the conviction that children can and should be classified at an early age, according to inborn intellectual differences, that underlay the entire remodelling of the school system at this time. Another example may be found in the later report by the Consultative Committee, *The Primary School* (1931). By this time separate junior schools were increasing in number as a result of 'Hadow reorganisation' and in advocating methods of internal organisation full reliance was again placed on the evidence of psychological witnesses. A memorandum printed as an appendix to the report gave Burt's advice to the Committee:

> From the point of view of educational organisation one of the most important facts revealed by intelligence tests is the wide range of individual differences, and its steady expansion from year to year. . . . Older children, therefore, differ far more widely in intellectual capacity than younger children. During the infant period they can be grouped together without much regard to their different degrees of mental endowment. At the age of eight or nine, however, to put together in a single room all those who are of the same age would be to organise a class that was extremely heterogeneous. By the age of ten, the children of a single age-group must be spread over at least three different standards. And by the age of twelve the range has become so wide, that a still more radical classification is imperative. Before this age is reached children need to be grouped according to their capacity, not merely in separate classes or standards, but in separate types of schools.

Accepting this argument, as it had earlier done in 1926, the Committee stressed the need for streaming—that is, classification, or differentiation, by ability—within the junior school. The break at eleven, far from seeming a mere administrative convenience, now appeared as an educational measure of first importance to be exploited in full:

> The break at the age of eleven has rendered possible a more thorough classification of children. *It is important that this opportunity should be turned to the fullest account.* One great advantage of the self-contained primary school is that the teachers have special opportunities for making a suitable classification of the children according to their natural gifts and abilities.

In accordance with the advice received from their psychological witnesses, the Committee went on to advocate, wherever possible, a 'triple track system of organisation, viz: a series of "A" classes or groups for the bright children, and a series of smaller "C" classes or groups to include retarded children, both series being parallel to the ordinary series of "B" classes or groups for the average children' (Hadow, 1931, 257-8, 77-8). This advice was frequently followed, in schools that were sufficiently large, the 'A' class being directed towards the 'scholarship'. Thus the existence of a separate system of secondary education, with a strictly selective entry, greatly influenced the development of the basic units in the national system of education. A pattern previously imposed on the school system as a whole was now increasingly imposed within the schools themselves, often determining the nature of the education given to children from the age of seven or eight. As separate post-primary schools came into being,

14

these also, with official encouragement, adopted this method of internal organisation.

The 'multilateral' school and the Spens report

This growing emphasis on differentiation did not go without challenge. Already in 1925 the Association of Assistant Masters, the majority of whose members taught in secondary schools, passed unanimously a resolution at an annual conference in favour of secondary education for all—in one type of school. 'If secondary schools of various types were set up,' said the mover of the amendment for a unified school, 'it would mean that there would be in secondary schools of the present type a class which was bound to be looked upon as something socially superior to the children who would attend the new schools of the distinct types' (*The A.M.A.*, January, 1925). This probably the first declaration of support for a common secondary school by a teachers' organisation in England.

The kind of school the Assistant Masters had in mind was at that time called a 'multiple bias' or, later, a 'multilateral' (many-sided) school. There was acceptance that children differed in their intelligence, interests and rates of learning. The argument was that these differences could best be provided for in the single school, common to all, by the provision of different biasses or 'sides', and that this would be socially more acceptable than separating the children into different types of school. The idea, even then, was not a new one. The United States had already developed an 'end-on' system of common schools based on somewhat similar principles. Throughout Western Europe a movement for the unification of education was gaining support—partly as an aspect of the drive towards 'equality of opportunity'. In Germany this took the form of pressure for the *Einheitschule*; in France, for the *École*

Unique. In all these countries the single school was seen as providing a variety of directions or courses to meet the needs of different groups of children.

There were other bodies which, in the 1920s and 1930s, saw the need for unification rather than further differentiation, including the Associations of Assistant Mistresses and of Headmistresses. In 1928 the Board of Education's policy of preserving the secondary schools inviolate was condemned by the National Union of Teachers in which teachers in elementary schools predominated. In *The Hadow Report and After* the union called for experiments with 'the large multiple bias school' suggesting that authorities be permitted to establish these, 'and even encouraged to do so' (p. 34). A year later the National Association of Labour Teachers published an important statement entitled *Education, a Policy*, which proposed that all post-primary education should be based on multilateral schools. At this time Godfrey Thomson, an influential educational psychologist, contributed his view in *A Modern Philosophy of Education* (1929). Drawing on experience of teaching in the United States, this was apparently the first important educational work published in this country to use the American term 'comprehensive' for the single secondary school. 'The social solidarity of the whole nation,' wrote Thomson, 'is more important than any of the defects to which a comprehensive high school may be subject' (p. 274).

Increasing support was forthcoming in the 1930s when the Consultative Committee, now under the chairmanship of Sir Will Spens, was asked to report on secondary education, with special reference to 'technical high schools'. In evidence submitted to the committee in 1934 the Trades Union Congress advocated the single school with grammar and 'modern' sides. A year later the National Union of Teachers, in its evidence, suggested that 'differentiated studies in the same school' would be 'the ideal arrangement', asking for the common secondary school where size permitted (N.U.T., 1935, 13, 20). In the same year important future developments were heralded in a headline in *The Schoolmaster* (30 May 1935): 'Secondary Education for All: London makes history.' The London Labour Party had declared its support for the multilateral school as early as 1932, and the headline referred to the report of a sub-committee of the London County Council set up in July, 1934. This advocated 'a new kind of secondary school', multilateral in character. Although it was legally impossible at this stage to set up the single school, in view of the different statutory regulations then governing elementary and secondary education, the L.C.C. remained an advocate of the multilateral school.

The Spens Report was published late in 1938. Taking the Hadow recommendations a stage further it proposed that all 'post-primary' schools should become full secondary schools, administered under the secondary code. But it rejected proposals for a unified secondary school. Once again the advice of psychological witnesses provided the basis for this rejection and the alternative proposals. 'General intelligence', the committee had been told, is 'the most important factor in determining [the child's] work in the classroom'; moreover this factor could be 'approximately' measured by administering intelligence tests. 'We were informed,' runs the report, 'that, with few exceptions, it is possible at a very early age to predict with some degree of accuracy the ultimate level of a child's intellectual powers.' Since these evidently varied, 'different children from the age of eleven, if justice is to be done to their varying capacities, require types of education varying in certain important respects' (Spens, 1938, 123-5). Secondary education should be provided in three types of school, the grammar school (a term now introduced anew), the technical school (derived from the junior technical schools started in 1912), and the modern school (as advocated in the Hadow Report of 1926 but yet to be established in many areas).

These findings were challenged, as the Hadow recommendations had been but on a considerably larger scale, by both teachers' associations and other bodies. The main objection was voiced by the Trades Union Congress: 'The separation of the three types of school is . . . bound to perpetuate the classification of children into industrial as well as social strata. . . . So long as this stratification of children at the age of eleven remains, it is in practice useless to talk of parity in education or equality of opportunity in later life.' Proposing the establishment of multilateral schools the T.U.C. stressed that this was 'the only way of bringing about educational parity and that approach to social and industrial equality which we may properly expect our education system to contribute to the society in which we live' (T.U.C., 1939). This point of view was gaining support when war broke out in the autumn of 1939.

An open question

It would be wrong to lay too great stress on the opposition between those who advocated a single secondary school and those who supported a variety of types of school during the years up to 1940. Advocates of the single school tended to accept current theories about the need for differentiating children from an early age, and sharply after the age of eleven, hence their support for bringing 'sides' together under one roof in a multilateral school—a conception rather different, as we shall see, from that of the comprehensive school as it developed in the 1950s. Advocates of a variety of types of school, of the overriding need to differentiate, also stressed the need for unification. The first Hadow report (1926) spoke of the need for 'a broad common foundation' though provided in different schools. The Spens Committee, advocating a full secondary education for all on tripartite lines, stressed the need for parity of conditions as between schools. While regarding 'the general adoption of the multilateral idea' as 'too subversive a change . . . in a long established system', even as the goal of a long-term policy, they nevertheless held that 'the multilateral idea, though it may not be expressed by means of the multilateral school, should permeate the system of secondary education as we conceive it'. Experiments with multilateral schools might be undertaken in thinly populated areas, or 'areas of new population', and especially in Wales where there had been a vocal demand for the common school (Spens, 1938, 201-2, 345).

After the first summaries of its findings, the Spens Report created little stir outside the educational world. In a debate on the recommendations in the Commons, in February, 1939, only two members spoke in favour of the multilateral school, one Labour, one Conservative. W. G. Cove, ex-president of the N.U.T. and a leading member of the National Association of Labour Teachers which had for long advocated the multilateral school, described this as a 'microcosm of real democracy'. Annesley Somerville, a master at Eton from 1885 to 1922 and a prominent Conservative back-bencher—now in his eighties—strongly supported the multilateral solution. In reply to doubts about the necessary size of such schools, expressed in the Spens Report, he pointed to the 1,100 boys at Eton where, he said, there was 'the greatest amount of individualism'. As for 'multilateralism', he went on, 'I agree with that. I think it is far better than what they propose . . . I would recommend the gradual introduction of the multilateral system.' Replying to the debate Kenneth

Lindsay, Parliamentary Secretary to the Board of Education, said that this was not a matter on which the Board could 'make up its mind next week or the week after'. The issue remained open, but no effective step could possibly be taken until the old division between elementary and secondary education was superseded and successive primary and secondary stages established as the future pattern, as had been proposed by the Hadow Committee thirteen years earlier.

A notable feature of the inter-war period was the way in which a uniform system of education was patterned. Official committees, appointed by the President of the Board of Education from names suggested by permanent officials, worked out the lines of policy from which succeeding governments selected those aspects they were prepared to implement. This was to continue an approach which was characteristic of the development of the educational system as a whole, as was pointed out by Sir Fred Clarke, principal of the Institute of Education and London University. In an influential book *Education and Social Change*, published just after the outbreak of war, he wrote:

> The mass of the English people have never yet evolved schools of their own. Schools have always been provided for them from above, in a form and with a content of studies that suited the ruling interests . . . Hitherto there has appeared no sure sign of the growth of a genuine popular philosophy of education which would seize upon the elementary school and make it the instrument of its own clearly conceived social and cultural purpose (pp. 30-31).

Clarke was particularly concerned with the consequent divisions in post-primary education which contrasted with his experience over many years of the more open systems in the Dominions.

2

The War and the Education Act, 1939-44

The need for reform

On Sunday, 3 September, 1939, Britain declared war on Germany. Before the second world war ended a new Education Act was to be placed on the statute book opening new perspectives for educational advance. But before considering this, it will be as well to take stock. What was the actual position at the close of the inter-war period?

In 1938, the last full year before the war, 88 per cent of children aged five to fourteen in England and Wales attended public elementary schools; of these 79 per cent left at fourteen to go straight out to work, more often than not into blind alley occupations. Of the children over eleven in public elementary schools, 63 per cent were in reorganised senior departments or 'modern' schools, but as many as 37 per cent were still in the senior classes of all-age schools, and their education correspondingly restricted. The difference in conditions provided for elementary and secondary school pupils was marked; the cost per pupil in the secondary school was twice that for pupils in elementary schools, while the capital cost of providing a place in a secondary school was three times as great as that for the elementary school.

There was still a long way to go before even a formal equality of opportunity could be said to exist. Not only did conditions differ, but the salaries of teachers in elementary schools were lower than for those in secondary schools—there were, in fact, two separate salary scales. The size of classes differed, the elementary schools suffering from much overcrowding. Fees were still charged in secondary schools; over half of these charged between nine and fifteen guineas a year, sufficient to keep out the bulk of working-class children—some charged more. In 1938, there were 470,000 pupils in secondary schools, 11·3 per 1,000 of the population (in 1920 a Departmental Committee had proposed that 20 per 1,000 of the population was the immediately necessary target). Of these, 43·4 per cent paid full fees, 9·7 per cent paid partial fees, and 46·9 per cent received their secondary education free. On the eve of the war, only 12 per cent of public elementary school pupils proceeded, at the age of ten or eleven, to secondary schools (some of these as fee-payers) (*Education in 1938*). At this time it was calculated that whereas one pupil in eight from a 'public' school gained a place at a university, only one in 150 from an elementary school did so. Towards the close of the 1930s there was mounting evidence, from both psychologists and sociologists, exposing the wastage of ability consequent upon so divided and restricted a system of education. Already before the war the determination was growing of bringing about a radical change in the structure of the system.

Prelude to legislation

During the early years of the war what had been relatively scattered calls for educational advance became a steadily growing demand for 'a new order' in English education. From 1941—a most critical point in the early years of the war—preparations were made for a new and far-reaching Education Act.

During this century no great Act of Parliament affecting education has ever been passed in an era of peace; the Education Act of 1902 followed on the Boer war, that of 1918 was passed in the closing stages of what was then known as the Great War, while the 1944 Act also was passed before the second world war ended. In wartime aspirations are heightened, and, as the whole population is involved, and there is to this extent equality of sacrifice, there is much wider recognition of the justice of providing equality of opportunity. If maximum effort during the war is to be maintained, then it must seem worth that effort in terms of what the country will offer its people in the future, and so governments are stimulated to work out plans. Moreover, in wartime there is often rapid scientific and industrial change, so that the need for educational change is seen in a new light, while the objections of those who deplore undue expenditure are correspondingly lessened.

In such circumstances, much of the argument and discussion attending educational reform in peacetime falls away as irrelevant and there can be something of a breakthrough, a growing consensus of opinion on key points rather than preoccupation with minor modifications.

In 1941 discussions already under way were brought to a point with the issue by the Board of Education, of a memorandum entitled 'Education after the War'. This was not published but circulated privately to many organisations as a basis for discussion; it became known, by its cover, as the 'Green Book'. Opinions were asked for and, during the next two years, over a hundred reports and memoranda, from organisations of all kinds, flowed into the Board making proposals about every facet of educational policy. Books and pamphlets appeared in growing numbers and many conferences and meetings centred on different aspects of the educational system. In the course of these exchanges the multilateral school was more widely discussed than ever before.

The lines of official thinking, however, were already apparent from the 'Green Book' which, while accepting the Hadow policy of secondary education for all over the age of eleven, unequivocally advocated a tripartite system of secondary schools as put forward by the Spens report. ' "Equality of opportunity" does not mean that all children should receive the same form of education,' runs the relevant section. 'At the secondary stage there must be ample variety of educational opportunity.' This view was to be firmly maintained by the Board of Education throughout the war, and in the crucial period of reconstruction immediately following it. It was, however, more strongly challenged in the 1940s than it had been earlier.

With the formation of a national government in 1940, Labour and Liberal ministers now entered the government alongside the Conservatives. The Labour Party, therefore, spoke with a new authority when, at its annual conference in 1942, it gave official party support to the multilateral school. On behalf of the National Executive, a resolution calling for 'the development of a new type of multilateral school which could provide a variety of courses suited to children of all normal types' was moved by Harold Clay. 'We advocate the application of the common school principle,' he declared. 'We believe that it is sound that every child in the State should go to the same kind of school' (Labour Party, 1942). To this view the Trades Union Congress lent its support proposing in a 'Memorandum on Education after the War', that the Board of Education should 'undertake really substantial experiments in the way of multilateral schools' (T.U.C. 1942).

It was not only Labour organisations that stressed this point, others to do so included the Society of Friends, the English New Education Fellowship—an influential organi-
24

sation of progressive educationists—as well as the London County Council and some Welsh county councils.

There were clearly fundamental differences about the future pattern of secondary education, but this was only one point among many vital ones, and tended to take a subsidiary place. The Council of Educational Advance, which was established in 1942 by the Trades Union Congress, the Cooperative Union Education Committee, the National Union of Teachers and the Workers' Educational Association, conducted an energetic campaign on more general issues rather than for the common secondary school. It emphasised the need for a genuine secondary education for all by raising the standards of all post-primary schools to the level of the existing secondary schools and abolishing fees. This was the standpoint taken up by the County Councils Association, the Association of Directors and Secretaries for Education, and several teachers' associations including the Incorporated Association of Headmasters and the N.U.T., and it was on these points that a general consensus developed. A resolution passed by the annual conference of the N.U.T. in 1944, for example, urged the Board of Education 'to ensure that there should be parity of conditions in respect of premises, amenities, staffing, and the size of classes in every type of school' (*Education*, 28 April, 1944).

Many organisations, then, accepted that secondary schools should be of different types, holding that, if each had equivalent amenities, each would be of equal status. Children would be allocated to these different schools according to their 'abilities'; in this sense equality of opportunity would be ensured. It was already noticeable, for instance, that the teachers' associations had grown more cautious in their attitude to the multilateral school; even the A.M.A. now decided that, while there was 'a great deal to be said' for this form of organisation, they were 'not prepared to say that multilateralism should occupy the whole field' (*The A.M.A.*, January, 1943, p. 24).

Some educationists, however, were now strong supporters of the common secondary school, and this did much to focus informed discussion. H. C. Dent, the influential editor of the *Times Educational Supplement*, was at this time a leading advocate of 'a new order'—to propose mere 'modification of the existing set-up is to talk in terms of a palliative, not a cure'. The existing system was 'both quantitatively and qualitatively grossly inadequate to meet the needs of a democracy'. Indeed, it represented 'the very essence of inequality of opportunity. It is socially stratified to a degree that would be ludicrous were it not so tragic'. What was required was the single common school. 'However much children may differ in character, temperament, ability, and aptitude, I am utterly opposed to the idea of segregating adolescents in different types of school', or, for that matter, he added, to 'segregating them on the score of ability in different classes in the same school. . . . All should be members of the one school, which should provide adequately for diversity of individual aptitudes and interests, yet unite all as members of a single community' (Dent, 1942, 14, 57-8). This was to add support to the view advanced by Sir Fred Clarke in his study *Education and Social Change* already (1940) referred to. Clarke based his argument on the nature of the English tradition in education and the changing needs of society. In Clarke's view the divisions in post-primary education were based on social and economic, not on educational considerations.

In the early years of the war, then, discussion of this key issue was well under way. Writing in 1942, Dent recorded 'at least a strong minority opinion (latterly growing increasingly in strength)' in favour of the multilateral school (Dent, 1942, 58). But there were distinguished educationists who argued strongly against this conception.

Among these were Clarke's predecessor as Director of the London Institute of Education—Sir Percy Nunn. As a member of a sub-committee which drafted the Hadow report of 1926 and, according to Burt (1959), the author of its main proposals concerning differentiation, he was profoundly out of sympathy with the concept of the common school, warning against the creation of a 'featureless mediocrity' (*Journal of Education*, February 1943). Another influential opponent was I. L. Kandel, a Mancunian with long experience as an educator in the United States, who had given evidence to the Spens Committee. Kandel argued that the common school would lead to the destruction of excellence; like Nunn, he felt it was essential to maintain the grammar school as a separate institution for the education of an élite of intelligence.

The White Paper and the Norwood Report, 1943

In 1943, when severe defeats were being inflicted on the Axis powers and the end of the war seemed in sight, the government began to turn its attention seriously to post-war reconstruction. In July the Board of Education issued a White Paper, *Educational Reconstruction*, as the formal preliminary to submitting a bill to Parliament. This document reflected the general tenor of criticisms in an unequivocal statement:

> There is nothing to be said in favour of a system which subjects children at the age of eleven to the strain of a competitive examination on which, not only their future schooling, but their future careers may depend.

But, having made this concession, it went on to describe the future system of secondary education for all as a tripartite system on the Spens model, which necessarily involved selection (or 'allocation') at the age of eleven.

'Such, then, will be the three main types of secondary school', the argument concluded, 'to be known as grammar, modern and technical schools'. There should be free interchange between different types, however, and perhaps, in certain circumstances, a combination of all on one site or in one building (pp. 6, 9-10).

On this occasion there was considerably more support for the multilateral school when the question was debated in the Commons. What was to be a prevailing pattern in future arguments was forecast by the Conservative President of the Board, R. A. Butler, when he replied:

I would say to those idealists who want to see more than one form of secondary education in the same school —sometimes called multilateral schools—that I hope that more than one type of secondary education may from time to time be amalgamated under one roof (*Hansard*, 29 July 1943).

Almost immediately the matter was translated to a new stage with the publication of a full-scale report on *Curriculum and Examinations in Secondary Schools*—produced this time not by a consultative committee but a special committee of the Secondary Schools Examinations Council under the chairmanship of Sir Cyril Norwood, former headmaster of Harrow. The procedure whereby this subcommittee had been invited to report, and the nature of its recommendations, aroused sharp criticism, not only from advocates of a unified secondary education but from educationists generally and psychologists in particular. This committee, by contrast with earlier ones, had not sought any advice from psychologists but based its recommendations on particular views about the nature of the child. The educational system, it affirmed, had 'thrown up' three 'rough groupings' of children with different 'types of mind'. These were, first, 'the pupil who is interested in

28

learning for its own sake, who can grasp an argument or follow a piece of connected reasoning'; second, 'the pupil whose interests and abilities lie markedly in the field of applied science or applied art'; third, the pupil who 'deals more easily with concrete things than with ideas . . . abstractions mean little to him. . . . His horizon is near and within a limited area his movement is generally slow' (Norwood, 1943, 2-3). For these three groups of pupils three types of secondary school were needed—grammar, technical and modern schools.

Here was theoretical support of a new kind for the official Board of Education policy; and the arguments carried considerable weight. On the other hand the Norwood Report, as it became known, alerted many who had not hitherto been suspicious about the future of a real secondary education for all. An historian of education has expressed himself strongly on the arguments used, as others did at the time: 'Seldom has a more unscientific or more unscholarly attitude disgraced the report of a public committee,' wrote S. J. Curtis. The suggestion 'seems to be that the Almighty has benevolently created three types of child in just those proportions which would gratify educational administrators' (Curtis, 1952, 144).

Among the public bodies which produced an immediate reply was the London County Council which had been seriously considering the matter since 1935. The Norwood Committee's arguments, it suggested, were little more than 'a clever piece of rationalisation'. The three different types of post-primary schools had 'emerged as a result of an educational system based far more on social and economic factors than on the psychology of children'. The disadvantages of a divided secondary system were outlined:

The prime difficulty about accepting such a tripartite system of secondary education is that, if it be accepted, the secondary school of the future will, in effect, consist of two select types—an academic and a technical type —together with the 'rest' left behind in a large group of 'modern' schools. Though this would be an advance on the present arrangement, particularly if all three types are provided with the same amenities, it would remain true that modern schools will be places which all or many will try to avoid. The existence of two favoured and select types relatively small in number alongside 'the rest' in a large number of schools will make the problem of selection and re-selection at eleven and thirteen a much more serious matter than it need be (*T.E.S.*, 4 December 1943).

The objections of psychologists were summarised by Cyril Burt, whose advocacy of early differentiation and selection rested on the theory of innate differences of intelligence, rather than of aptitudes (for instance, technical aptitudes). The apparent endorsement by the Norwood report of 'qualitatively different aptitudes producing qualitatively different types' of children was, he said, a theory as outmoded as phrenology.

This view entirely reverses the facts as they are now known to us. . . . The proposed allocation of all children to different types of school at the early age of eleven cannot provide a sound psychological solution . . . the grounds for [so doing] are administrative rather than psychological (Burt, 1943, 131, 140).

The Education Act, 1944. A new phase

It was during these months, when there was a growing realisation that the future pattern of secondary education was a key question, that the Education Bill was being drafted. Introduced into the House of Commons on 16 December 1943, it received the royal assent on 4 August

1944. During these eight months there had been much debate and in its final form the Act made no mention of types of secondary school. On the other hand the relevant clause was clearly based on the long prevailing outlook as to the nature of 'abilities' and the need for variety of provision:

> The schools available for an area shall not be deemed sufficient unless they are sufficient in number, character and equipment to afford for all pupils opportunities for education offering such variety of instruction and training as may be desirable in view of their different ages, abilities and aptitudes, and of the different periods for which they may be expected to remain at school.

If these words suggest that a tripartite system was in mind—and Butler made his support for this clear in Parliament—the multilateral system could also now be legally established. It was later claimed that this compromise was due to the pressure of the Labour Party and other interested bodies (*Labour Party*, 1950, 94-5). However this may be, attention had already been drawn to this possibility, when the Bill was under discussion, by an experienced educational administrator, J. Chuter Ede, the Labour Parliamentary Secretary to the Board. 'I do not know where people get the idea about three types of school,' he said, in a speech in April, 1944, 'because I have gone through the Bill with a small tooth comb, and I can find only one school for senior pupils and that is a secondary school. What you like to make of it will depend on the way you serve the precise needs of the individual area in the country' (*The Times*, 14 April 1944).

The 1944 Education Act made great changes in the structure of English education. Secondary education for all children was established, as an integral part of an educational system which was seen as a 'continuous process' ranging

31

from the primary school to further or higher education. The school leaving age was raised to fifteen, though this was not implemented until 1947, and provision was made for a further rise to sixteen 'as soon as the Minister is satisfied that it has become practicable'; this latter step had not been taken twenty years later, though by then it was generally agreed to be indispensable. In addition the structure of local authorities in education was re-organised to eliminate the small 'Part III' authorities which, since the 1902 Act, had been responsible for elementary education alone; as a result each of the 146 authorities now had control over both primary and secondary education. All were required to prepare and submit development plans to the new Ministry of Education—which now had powers 'to control and direct' the implementation of educational policy. These plans, estimating and meeting the educational needs of each area, were to be submitted to the Ministry within one year.

While formidable administrative and financial difficulties remained, it was now open to the determined local education authority to submit plans for the establishment of the unified secondary school—still called the multi-lateral school. Already the Education Committee of the L.C.C. was hard at work for it was faced with the task of replacing a large proportion of its schools which had been destroyed by bombing. Two weeks before the Education Act passed into law it produced its report, and this was accepted by the full council on 1 August 1944. This proposed the reorganisation of most of London's secondary schooling on a unified system in single schools. With the passing of the Education Act and the L.C.C. decision, the pre-history of the comprehensive school ends, and a new stage begins.

3

The Tripartite system of secondary education, 1945-52

Education and social advance

In July 1945, two months after the ending of the war with Germany, there took place the first general election for ten years. For the first time in its history the Labour Party was returned with a majority—of nearly 200—over all other parties. It was an unexpectedly large majority vote for a policy of industrial and social reconstruction, for the party's policy had included nationalisation of the mines and of steel, the establishment of a national health service, and other measures of social welfare affecting pensions, town planning, housing and education. There were, however, economic difficulties—the capital equipment of industry was run down, the country was deeply in debt to the United States, the balance of payments adverse. The general election of 1950 saw the almost complete erosion of the Labour majority while another election a year later brought in the Conservative party, which was to remain in power for thirteen years.

In spite of economic difficulties, much of the Labour programme was carried out after 1945; in particular full employment was maintained—in sharp contrast to the inter-war position—and, in spite of a wage freeze which lasted till 1948, wages rose and productivity increased, albeit slowly. The importance of education to economic advance and social welfare was more widely recognised than before the war; one of the most significant advances was the doubling of the number of university students in three years—between 1944 and 1947. Another new factor was the heightened aspirations of new sections for a systematic education leading to wider opportunities; skilled workers in particular, it was shown by various sociological surveys, were now increasingly demanding a grammar school education for their children. The intense pressure on the 'secondary' schools after the first world war was now paralleled by a new pressure on the free 'grammar' schools, the products of the 1944 Act.

The pattern of provision—local authority development plans

In this situation the two conflicting tendencies in secondary education traced in Chapter 1 reasserted themselves—towards differentiation on the one hand, and towards unification on the other. The Act had laid down no rules governing the pattern of the provision to be made. Local authorities, whose plans for educational reconstruction were often linked to plans for urban reconstruction—as was the intention—now began to work out their development plans. Some, for instance, London, Southend and Oldham, proposed the single secondary school, the multilateral or, as it was now called in London, the comprehensive school; others, the majority, followed the advice of the Spens and Norwood Committees and proposed the tripartite solution. A number straddled the two, proposing a number of 'bilateral' schools of various types, grammar-modern, technical-modern, or technical-grammar; but these were originally seen simply as two of the three orthodox types' under one roof.

In spite of these differences the period 1945-51 saw the

tripartite system firmly established—the advocates of the comprehensive school in this period making little headway. There were a number of reasons for this. For one thing the different types of school—grammar, technical and modern—already existed. The junior technical schools of the 1920s and '30s admittedly recruited at thirteen rather than eleven, and provided for only 3 per cent of the age group. But it was a comparatively simple administrative matter gradually to lower their age of recruitment and to plan some expansion. Many authorities had not completed the reorganisation of their all-age elementary schools before the war and this was now seen as urgent, since post-primary education in all-age schools was not classed as 'secondary' under the 1944 Act, and it was the plain duty of local authorities to implement the Act and provide secondary education for all their children over eleven. Then, in 1947 came the raising of the school leaving age which brought another 400,000 pupils into the schools and involved planning, building and equipment. Under these circumstances it is, perhaps, not surprising that many local authorities tended to concentrate on immediate necessities, accepting the structure that had developed and abjuring any idea of radical change.

As has been noted, the Education Act had greatly strengthened the power of the Minister of Education, and it had been laid down that all local development plans must be 'approved'. Throughout this period the influence of the Ministry was continuously brought to bear on local authorities engaged on drawing up their plans. Already in December 1945—very shortly after the end of the war—the Ministry informed local authorities that 'for the immediate purpose of planning, and in the light of the existing lay-out of schools' it was 'inevitable . . . at the outset to think in terms of the three types, and to include information of the amount of accommodation allocated to each type in the development plan' (Circular 73, 12 December 1945). Intentions were also made clear in the first pamphlet issued by the post-war Ministry (*The Nation's Schools*, 1945). This repeated the assumptions of the Norwood report, favouring 'three broad types' of secondary school to meet 'the differing needs of different pupils'. Indeed it took the argument further by saying that the modern school was intended for working-class children 'whose future employment will not demand any measure of technical skill and knowledge', and also suggested a reduction in the proportion of grammar school places. The introduction of the multilateral school, it argued, following Spens, should be limited to 'sparsely populated districts' though there might be 'judicious experiments' elsewhere.

Strong objections were made to this publication, voiced particularly at the Labour Party conference, so that the Minister of Education, Ellen Wilkinson, announced that it would not be reprinted. But the same general policy remained, in outline, in *A Guide to the Educational System of England and Wales* (1945), the second pamphlet to be published by the Ministry, and the pamphlet which eventually replaced *The Nation's Schools* differed little from its predecessor. *The New Secondary Education* (1947), as this was called, once more summarised the Norwood Committee's theories about the three types of mind, and stressed the need for the corresponding three types of school. This pamphlet clearly represented the Ministry's views over a considerable period, and was reprinted unaltered as late as 1958.

The 'trend from multilateralism'

In assessing the establishment of the tripartite system after the war it must be remembered that the first purpose-built comprehensive schools in England were not opened until 1954. The resources for new school buildings of this type were not made available until the early 1950s. In the meantime, following the war, there developed something of a 'trend away from multilateralism' (Banks, 1955, 144). Grammar school teachers in particular, who had pioneered the concept of the 'multi-bias' school in the 1920s and '30s, now grew less enthusiastic. By according parity of conditions, the 1944 Act had, in the eyes of many grammar school teachers and heads, lowered the status of these schools vis-à-vis the modern schools and at the same time removed some of their independence. Their organisations now adopted an opposite policy and, worried by the potential threat to the survival of the grammar school as a separate institution, came out in open and sometimes bitter opposition to the new concept of the comprehensive school. Already, in February 1947, this view found forceful expression in an article by Eric James, High Master of Manchester Grammar School (a direct grant school), who argued that the common school would inevitably lead to 'grave social, educational and cultural evils' and 'may well be a national disaster' (T.E.S., 1 February 1947).

Two years later, in an influential book, James argued the case for a separate education for the intellectual élite; the common school, he said, would lead to 'a narrowing and impoverishment of the whole content of education' (James, 1949, 95). Professor Kandel argued on similar lines while the secretary of the Association of Education Committees, W. P. Alexander, commenting on Kandel's opposition, wrote that he found himself 'most completely in agreement' (Education, 16 January 1948). H. C. Dent was another who had second thoughts; he became a champion of the secondary modern school, and increasingly sceptical as to the advantages of comprehensive education which, he now claimed, ran counter to the English 'tradition of segregation' (Dent, 1952, 12). Finally the N.U.T., which, unlike the A.M.A., had never adopted the multilateral school as a definite policy—favouring experimentation—now took up a cautious attitude; an amendment to a motion at its 1948 conference proposing opposition to tripartism was declared 'very largely lost'.

What of the Labour Party, as apart from Labour ministers? Officially pledged by the decision of the annual conference of 1942 to support secondary organisation on multilateral lines, it reiterated this policy on several occasions. But the Minister of Education—Ellen Wilkinson —was unimpressed. 'People have said that by talking in terms of three types of school we are promulgating a wrong social philosophy,' she said in a speech in June 1946. 'I do not agree.' And she went on to argue that the right social philosophy was to regard all kinds of socially useful work as equal in value, and by implication all forms of secondary education. 'By abolishing fees in maintained schools we have ensured that entry to those schools shall be on the basis of merit. No one can truly say that grammar schools are being filled with children from a privileged social class. . . . Not everyone wants an academic education. After all, coal has to be mined and fields ploughed, and it is a fantastic idea that we have allowed, so to speak, to be cemented into our body politic, that you are in a higher social class if you add up figures in a book than if you plough the fields and scatter the good seed on the land' (*Education*, 21 June 1946).

George Tomlinson, who shortly succeeded as Minister, did not argue in this way and did approve various schemes which included proposals for individual comprehensive schools. But he did not break free from the prevailing pattern. Both he and his parliamentary secretary, D. R. Hardman, found frequent occasion to praise grammar schools and deprecate 'tampering' with them; the form in which

38

opposition to the comprehensive school now more frequently found expression. At the Labour Party conference in 1947 a resolution deprecating this policy was passed and the Minister urged 'to take great care that he does not perpetuate under the new Education Act the undemocratic tradition of English secondary education'; the need for 'the rapid development' of the common secondary school was stressed. But many important matters came up for consideration at this time, and long term educational developments were still in what may be called the planning stage. Only those fully engaged at the local level, on education committees or as school governors, were really aware of the far-reaching decisions that could be taken at this time. Moreover not a few Labour councillors and aldermen were themselves products of local grammar schools, or among those who had fought hard to open up the secondary schools since the 1920s, and they had come to see transfer to an academic school as the way to success for the working-class child which should not, accordingly, be superseded. In any case, many authorities with Labour majorities made no more than a token bow towards the comprehensive school in their eventual plans.

The matter was first brought into the open at a national level when, in 1949, various proposals for comprehensive schools were turned down, in particular, the plan from Middlesex where the Labour council advocated a fully comprehensive system. 'All children are not alike, either in their aptitudes or in their standards of ability,' wrote Tomlinson in a letter to the county council rejecting the plan. 'There are broad groups of children who can suitably be handled together.' When the Labour government fell in 1951 the *Times Educational Supplement*—now under a new editor and henceforth strongly opposed to the comprehensive school—wrote approvingly that it was 'extremely doubtful whether Mr. Tomlinson ever once lifted.

a hand' to increase the number of comprehensive schools (19 October 1951).

Although a number of plans put forward by local authorities for individual comprehensive schools were approved at this time, the system that was developed in these years was the tripartite system as originally outlined by the Spens Committee and developed in theory by the Norwood report and by the pamphlets issued by the Ministry of Education. Each type of school was seen as having a particular function, yet each was to have parity of conditions. In theory each child was to be 'allocated' to the type of school serving his particular needs; in practice the selection examination at eleven plus rapidly became even more competitive than it had been before the war since only the grammar (and some technical) schools provided an extended education and an avenue to the universities and the professions.

It is clear that the intention, at this stage, was to develop a neat administrative structure with the grammar schools running a seven-year course (11-18) for most of their pupils (as outlined in the Ministry's pamphlet *The Road to the Sixth Form*, 1951), technical schools arranged in parallel and transformed from the pre-war thirteen to fifteen schools to the full seven years (as outlined in the Spens Report which had concentrated specifically on the need for technical high schools of this type), and modern schools with a four-year, and eventually a five-year course (11-16). The Spens Committee had suggested that 15 per cent of an age-group were fit for a grammar school education, that technical high schools should be developed and extended, and that the rest of the children—some 70-80 per cent, should go to modern schools (Spens, 1938, 322-3).

In practice there were difficulties in working out this scheme. Local authorities were chary of developing technical schools. Whether this was because, due to the equipment required, they were particularly expensive, or whether it was because of confusion as to their function is unclear. But as late as 1958 secondary technical schools still contained under 4 per cent of the relevant age-groups while many authorities had none at all. The system that developed was, therefore, to all intents and purposes, a bipartite system consisting of grammar schools on the one hand and modern schools on the other, the former taking, in 1950, 20 per cent of the age group.

Selection and the secondary modern school

With the abolition of fees in grammar schools, the educational justification for this division lay in the theory of intelligence, as outlined in chapter one. Equality of opportunity, it was argued, had been achieved since every child had equal opportunity to obtain a place in a grammar school—finance no longer entered into the question. A system of 'objective' examinations determined who would gain these places, and, although the nature of this examination, or system of selection, varied from authority to authority, in general it comprised tests in intelligence, English and arithmetic, so that (it was argued) those with the ability to profit from a grammar school education received one, while those shown to be without this ability received an education better adapted to their needs in a secondary modern school. The system of selection was officially regarded as fair and indeed as scientific, and a great deal of energy and money was expended in an attempt to make these tests as valid as possible. The National Foundation for Educational Research, established after the war, was largely concerned with the production of these tests, as was Moray House in Edinburgh.

Priority was necessarily accorded during these years, given this policy, to establishing the new system of secondary modern schools. Reorganisation meant that many new schools had to be built and these were added to the pre-war 'senior' or 'modern' schools to house the bulk of the 11-15 age-group. Modern schools were originally intended to be strictly demarcated from grammar and technical schools; they were to give a general education with a practical, but not a vocational bias—they were not to enter pupils for external examinations, least of all the School Certificate (as the grammar school examination was then called). 'Free from the pressure of any external examination' as the Ministry put it in *The Nation's Schools* (1945), 'these schools can work out the best and liveliest forms of secondary education suited to their pupils. It is essential that they should retain this invaluable freedom which the best of their predecessors have used to such advantage, and should be enabled to advance along the lines they themselves feel to be right.' 'Freedom and flexibility,' it was reiterated in *The New Secondary Education* (1947), are the essence of the modern school, 'and indeed its great opportunity.'

William Taylor, in *The Secondary Modern School* (1963), adopting a sociological approach, points to the 'vague generalities' in which official statements about the aims of secondary modern schools were couched in this period; these, he suggests, served to conceal that these schools were fundamentally designed for working-class children the vast majority of whom would, on leaving school, go straight out to work for which, at this time, no training and little educational qualifications were required. As we have seen, this had already been suggested in *The Nation's Schools*. However this may be, great efforts were made by the teachers in many of these schools to develop curricula and activities that would interest and motivate their pupils, often with success; these are described in H. C. Dent's book *Secondary Modern Schools* (1958).

42

Nevertheless the pressure for entry to the grammar schools constantly grew; in the eyes of parents as of the public generally the modern school never gained the 'parity of esteem' which, the Ministry held, 'it must secure by its own efforts' (*The New Secondary Education*). Taylor argues that this injunction was incapable of fulfilment, due to the social functions such schools were bound to serve (Taylor, 1963, 42-55). The system now developing was essentially élitist, or, as Michael Young put it later, meritocratic (*The Rise of the Meritocracy*, 1961). By 1950, one child in five transferred from the primary to the grammar school, compared to one in seven or eight before the war; and of those gaining a place in a grammar or technical school, one in eight went on directly to a university compared to one in 22,000 from a modern school. Inevitably junior schools were driven to stream their children as early as the age of seven in order to prepare the most advanced for the selection examination; streaming even penetrated the infant school. With important examinations in view the grammar schools themselves were streamed, operating on the same principle. The strict delimitation between types of school, characteristic of this period, imparted a severe rigidity to the entire system. Contrary influences, however, were already apparent.

The first plans for comprehensive schools

When local authorities first settled down to work out their development plans the idea of the multilateral school had considerable support among teachers, administrators and educationists. From the start, then, a number of authorities began to think in terms of the single secondary school.

By far the largest and most powerful of these was the London County Council which had already taken the decision to reorganise on comprehensive lines before the Act was passed. Adopted by the council in March, 1947, the London School Plan—an impressive volume—envisaged the establishment of 103 comprehensive schools, to cater for a high proportion of the secondary population of 190,000 children. Of these, 67 were to be full comprehensive schools, 36 to be 'county complements'—the intention was to pair the latter with existing 'aided' grammar schools which could not legally be extended as comprehensive schools.

The London School Plan was designed as the educational complement of the County of London Plan, which was concerned with the post-war reconstruction of the entire city. Education is a matter of 'all-round growth and development, physical, intellectual, social and spiritual', stated the L.C.C., 'and it seems indefensible to categorise schools on the basis of intellect only'. It was a matter of first rate importance for modern society 'that life in school should promote a feeling of social unity among adolescents of all kinds and degrees of ability'. This the comprehensive school was designed to do.

But London was not the only authority to produce plans for multilateral—or comprehensive—schools. Coventry, also badly damaged during the war, planned ten schools to cover some 80 per cent of pupils; Westmorland, a rural area, planned eight schools; Anglesey and the Isle of Man each proposed four schools to cater for all children of secondary age. A number of county boroughs, for instance Southend, Oldham, Reading, Bolton, and later Bradford planned for the single secondary school, while two of the most determined authorities, in this early stage, were the counties of Middlesex and the West Riding.

Some of these plans materialised, others did not. H. C. Dent, surveying the situation in 1949, showed that while few local authorities had so completely disregarded the advice of the Ministry of Education as to plan completely multilateral systems, nonetheless few wanted the tripartite system in its unadulterated state (Dent, 1949, 147-8). But for building and other restrictions, he wrote five years later, 'there would have been many more experiments with comprehensive and multilateral schools' (Dent, 1954, 80). To give one example, Oldham was never able to establish its comprehensive schools, owing to lack of building allocations.

It may be noted here that the Ministry was by now insisting that multilateral or comprehensive schools must be large schools of about 1,600 pupils. The argument (advanced in Circular 144, 16 June 1947) ran as follows. The multilateral school must provide effective education of all three types; to do this it needed as a minimum a ten form entry (300 pupils), divided into two grammar streams, two technical streams, and six or seven modern streams. Comprehensive schools, if they were to offer sufficient variety of courses, must be of the same size, although the terms grammar, technical and modern would not be used.

What happened to those authorities which did propose a fully comprehensive system? As already noted, Middlesex was among the first to express the aim of giving 'some earnest . . . to parents of the determination of the County Council to provide a real secondary education for all pupils of secondary school age' (*Education*, 23 August 1946). To this end it proposed a rapid transition to comprehensive education by making use at first of existing buildings, rather than waiting for entirely new, purpose-built, schools as Coventry intended to do. The plan, based to some extent on American experience (where only a minority of schools are large), envisaged relatively small schools—with from 570 to 850 pupils—which would provide a common curriculum for all children up to the age of thirteen or fourteen. The first new school buildings would be erected, it

45

was proposed, 'in the next year or two'. Here was a new concept of the comprehensive school, one radically different from the kind of 'multilateral' school envisaged by the Ministry—as a very large school providing different courses for different types of child. Unlike the London Plan, it also indicated how rapid could be the transition to comprehensive education if adaptations were made in a planned way. The Middlesex plan, therefore, aroused great interest. It was submitted to the Ministry in 1948. In January 1949, it was returned with a demand for a complete review on two main grounds—first, the schools proposed were too small, second, the logical way of dealing with different 'types' of children was by providing different 'types' of school; meanwhile, only two experimental schools were permitted—Mellow Lane and Mount Grace. A year earlier a proposal from the North Riding to establish five comprehensive schools had been rejected on similar grounds.

A few comprehensive schools, however, were established in the 1940s—the first of these in rural areas. In 1945 the ancient grammar school at Windermere, founded by local yeomen in the sixteenth century, was reorganised to serve the whole community. If this was the first comprehensive school in England it remained also the smallest, having only some 200 pupils (all boys). Today, serving a wider area, it is housed in new buildings on the shores of the lake.

Anglesey and the Isle of Man (which controls its own education and is not subject to the British Parliament) were the first authorities to develop complete systems of comprehensive education. In Anglesey the idea of the common school has a long history, but here it was also a question of completing Hadow reorganisation. In 1945 the county was served by four small grammar schools, two secondary modern schools (at Holyhead and Beaumaris), while the rest of the children over eleven remained scattered in small all-age village schools up and down the island. The simplest solution to implementing the Act and providing secondary education for all was to extend the existing grammar schools to take in all children from the area as had been done at Windermere, and this the authority proposed.

At Holyhead the grammar and modern schools, which faced each other across a road, were fused in 1949. Children over eleven, from other local village schools, were also taken in and a comprehensive school with about 1,000 pupils of both sexes formed. At Beaumaris the same course was taken while at Amlych (in 1952) and Llangefni (in 1953) new buildings were erected (as at Beaumaris later). These developments came to public notice when, in November 1952, the Anglesey County Council announced the abolition of the selection examination.

Much the same development took place in the Isle of Man, where reorganisation was completed as early as 1947. During these years the West Riding, whose development plan opened with a statement rejecting the tripartite approach, was able to establish only one comprehensive school—the Calder High School which opened in 1947 utilising a building put up just before the war; other comprehensive schools were also planned.

The first of the L.C.C. purpose-built schools—Kidbrooke —was not opened until 1954. But in the meantime the L.C.C. wished to gain experience of the problems involved and, in 1946-7, established five 'interim' comprehensive schools by merging selective central schools with modern schools and making use of existing buildings, each school comprising about 1,200 pupils. In the following year three more schools were formed in this way. These schools were well equipped and staffed and began to provide that variety of courses for older pupils now typical of comprehensive schools. These experimental schools, wrote the L.C.C. later, 'blazed a trail which has become a broad highway, and under conditions of great difficulty and in face of some hostility they carried out pioneer work of the utmost value' (L.C.C., 1961, 14). It was not, however, work which was very widely heard of at this time. Nor, of course, were any of the schools fully comprehensive in that no grammar school had been drawn in.

From the angle of supporters of the comprehensive school, then, progress was slow, though it was apparent that, if building restrictions were lifted, advance would be more rapid. While the tripartite system was dominant, within it a new type of school was taking shape, as yet only in its chrysalis stage. During this period the theoretical discussion continued unabated, but, with certain exceptions, this discussion could not be illuminated by reference to the practical experience of comprehensive schools, since these as yet scarcely existed. In 1947, however, the Advisory Council on Education in Scotland published its report entitled *Secondary Education*. This firmly rejected 'the tripartite organisation proposed for England'. Such a scheme was attractive from the standpoint of administrative tidiness but, the report added, 'the whole scheme rests on an assumption which teacher and psychologist alike must challenge—that children of twelve sort themselves out neatly into three categories to which these three types of school correspond. It is difficult enough to assess general ability at that age: how much harder to determine specific bents and aptitudes with the degree of accuracy that would justify this three-fold classification' (p. 31). The committee proposed that the comprehensive school should be the norm for developments in Scotland— according to longstanding tradition the 'omnibus' school, as it was called, taking in all pupils, had usually been the typical school in the rural areas. A similar point of view was put at this time in *Three Schools or One* (1948) by Lady Simon of Wythenshawe, onetime member of the Spens Committee with long experience of work on the Manchester Education Committee. She found both Scottish and American experience relevant and reversed the trend whereby the latter was normally used as an argument against the common school. In 1949 *The Future of Secondary Education in Wales* appeared, the report of the Advisory Council for the principality. It saw the comprehensive—or at least bilateral—school as the main form of secondary provision in rural areas, that is, for the Welsh counties.

1951—Attitudes harden

In October 1951 the Prime Minister, C. R. Attlee, dissolved Parliament. For twenty months the Labour government had held on with a hairbreadth majority. But the enthusiasm of 1945 had gone, and the government's programme seemed unclear. The Conservatives were now returned with a small majority, one they were to increase at both the next elections, in 1955 and 1959.

Nationally, the Conservative Party did not favour the comprehensive school. Locally there had been, at first, little objection; in Coventry there was no Conservative opposition to the plan for comprehensive schools and in London, while not subscribing to the full London Plan, Conservatives were, at first, willing to accept 'experiments'. Southend, which proposed a full comprehensive school plan in 1945, had a Conservative majority. Nevertheless by 1951 positions had hardened. Two years earlier, on winning control of the Middlesex County Council, the Conservatives had scrapped the Labour plan for comprehensive education. Conservatives now expressed fears of huge schools which might become 'soulless educational factories'. Winston Churchill, the Conservative leader, spoke for many of his party when, in the General Election of 1951, he stressed the need 'to safeguard the independence, the high standards and the traditions of the grammar schools' (*T.E.S.*, 19 October 1951). Spokesmen like Quintin Hogg and R. A. Butler emphasised the Hadow line of the 1920s, calling for a variety of types of secondary school.

To some extent party lines were now beginning to form, and during the next decade the political struggle was to sharpen. At this stage, however, the discussion was still largely carried on as an educational issue among educationalists, or sometimes as a matter of local politics, with the occasional conflict between local authority and central government. The comprehensive school did not figure in the 1950 election manifestoes and was a minor issue in the 1951 election. The Conservative Minister of Education, Florence Horsbrugh, while having 'strong reservations' about large comprehensive schools, was willing to allow 'limited experiments'—she would not allow a local authority to provide no form of secondary education other than comprehensive schools. In 1953 she accepted Coventry's plan with the proviso that the schools established be regarded as strictly experimental, the buildings erected capable of being split up into separate schools 'should this course be found desirable' (*Education*, 11 December 1953).

The Coventry plans did not involve the absorption of any grammar schools. In London, however, plans for Kidbrooke school were well under way, and here a local girl's grammar school was to form part of the new comprehensive school. Miss Horsbrugh manifested her opposition to this step by refusing to allow this fusion to take place, although it had been approved by her predecessor, George Tomlinson. This decision resulted in an outcry including a clash in the House of Commons and a strong deputation of protest by the L.C.C. and by the Association of Education Committees representing all the local education authorities in the country. The Minister's action was seen as a blow at local autonomy in education. It was, however, an earnest of things to come.

4

New trends and expansion, 1953-62

The decade 1953-62 was one of change and development in English education, both in theory and in practice. During this period the number of pupils in the sixth forms of grammar schools more than doubled; many secondary modern schools established fifth forms for pupils staying on to take 'O' level in the General Certificate of Education, while, in 1962, a total of over 200,000 pupils were in schools classified as either comprehensive, multilateral, or bilateral. During these years, in the light of these developments, ideas about the nature of the child, and especially his capacity for learning, began to change. The fatalistic ideas which had dominated educational thinking and planning for a quarter of a century now met with strong criticism and attention turned from psychological justification of the existing system to sociological investigation of its effect.

Technological change and economic advance

The underlying cause of these developments is to be found in the new demands made on the educational system as a result of technological change and economic advance. Although Britain's rate of economic growth was low compared to most other advanced industrial countries, and although, due to recurrent balance of payments difficulties, the government pursued deflationary policies at roughly four-year intervals, the average rate of growth over the decade was just over 2 per cent (in terms of gross national product). As a result real incomes gradually increased and this in itself, as on previous occasions, led to a greater demand for education; aspirations were raised and so also the means of satisfying them. At the same time long term technological changes—more recently those connected with automation, sometimes characterised as the second industrial revolution—put a premium on skills and specialisation. This is shown in Table I, where the sharp decline in the number of unskilled workers is particularly striking :

TABLE I
Social Classes (males only) England and Wales
(in thousands)

Date	I Professional, etc	II Intermediate	III Skilled	IV Partly Skilled	V Unskilled
1931	336	1,855	6,848	2,552	2,459
1951	494	2,146	8,041	2,433	2,258
1961	591	2,368	7,933	3,237	1,422
Percentage increase, 1931-61	75.9	27.7	15.8	26.4	Minus 42.2

(*Sources:* 1951 Census, Occupational Tables, p. 666, Table D. 1961 Census, Occupational Tables, p. 125, Table 20. There are certain, but not significant, changes in category between 1951 and 1961.)

An important aspect of the technological revolution is the premium put on adaptability, itself a product of education, as well as the need for raising the educational level of the population as a whole, if technological advance is to be effectively implemented. 'The average worker in industry and commerce,' reported the Advisory Council for Education in 1959, 'requires much more education than was needed only a short time ago. . . . The growth in the proportion of highly skilled jobs, and the decline in the proportion of unskilled jobs, imply a reassessment of what must be attempted by people of only average intelligence. . . . It is not only at the top but almost to the bottom of the pyramid that the scientific revolution of our times needs to be reflected in a longer educational process' (Crowther, I, 123-4).

Such were the underlying trends at this time. But the secondary system as a whole remained within the framework established earlier which set strict limits to expansion. Grammar school places remained limited, modern schools were truncated, the eleven plus was a barrier restricting the access of the majority to a full secondary education. In the circumstances increasing pressure at first resulted in an intensification of the processes of streaming and selection. But it soon became apparent that the selective system so carefully consolidated since the war was bursting at the seams.

New developments in the secondary modern schools

In 1953 there were over a million pupils in secondary modern schools. In the official view, as we have seen, these schools were expected to work out a new approach to education; they were to base their curricula on the immediate experience and interests of the children who, it was held, gained more from practical activities than from abstract thinking and analysis. Such children, ran the theory at that time, lacked the innate intellectual capacity for a systematic secondary education.

A crucial aspect of this policy was that children in these schools should not enter for an external examination

But as early as 1946, many modern schools began actively to consider preparing pupils for the School Certificate, the grammar school examination taken at fifteen or sixteen which preceded the General Certificate of Education. Faced with the raising of the school leaving age to fifteen, in April 1947, this was naturally one of the ways chosen of making the extra year worthwhile. But in May 1946 this perspective was closed by the Ministry of Education which laid down regulations preventing schools other than grammar schools from entering pupils for *any* external examinations under the age of seventeen (Circular 103). Secondary modern pupils, therefore, were quite simply debarred from taking this examination unless they stayed at school two years above the new statutory leaving age.

The position remained unchanged until 1951 when the School Certificate was replaced by a new examination, the General Certificate of Education. Grammar schools wished to enter pupils from at least the age of fifteen and in response to pressure from them this was made the minimum age in 1953. Pupils could sit this examination in individual subjects, whereas a block of subjects had to be taken in the old School Certificate, but the standard of a pass was raised to the level that had formerly counted as a 'credit'. This, it was thought, would effectively put the examination beyond the range of any but grammar school pupils; though the lowering of the age of entry opened the way for entrants from modern schools, it was not expected that they would be forthcoming.

In a number of secondary modern schools, however, teachers encouraged pupils to stay on to sixteen and attempt the examination. From about 1953 the first G.C.E. successes by secondary modern school pupils began to be recorded. Some of these early results were remarkable in terms of the theories of the time.

It was the accepted view, for instance, that only a child

with an I.Q. of 115 or over could succeed in a grammar school; though, in practice, the I.Q. range taken into grammar schools varied with the proportion of places available in different areas. Secondary modern schools, however, entered children for G.C.E. whose recorded I.Q. at eleven had been 100 or less, and some of these children gained five or six passes in the G.C.E. five years later. One secondary modern school for girls in Middlesex, which took in only pupils who had failed to get into either a grammar or a selective central school, entered two girls in 1954 both of whom gained five passes; one had had an I.Q. of 97 on entry to the school, the other an I.Q. of 85 and a similarly low classification for English and arithmetic (Simon, 1955, 66). The first local authority to introduce G.C.E. courses into all its secondary modern schools, in 1953, was Bournemouth. By 1954, a year after the lowering of the age of entry, over 5,000 pupils from modern schools up and down the country were entered; by the summer of 1962 the figure had soared to 36,000.

The successful development of G.C.E. courses in secondary modern schools cast doubt on the validity of selection at eleven plus. This examination had been designed specifically for grammar schools and their pupils achieved an average pass rate for individual subjects of a little over 50 per cent. Yet here were secondary modern school pupils, rejected at eleven on the grounds of inadequate intellectual capacity, who had succeeded in the examination, and despite low I.Qs. It could now be argued that there was little logic in establishing two main types of school, grammar and modern, selecting carefully for the former, and then, through the establishment of 'G.C.E. streams' giving the same kind of education in each. The strict division between types of school, laid down as axiomatic after 1945, seemed no longer tenable. In reply it was suggested that children who were successful in modern schools would not have succeeded in grammar schools, where the teaching would not have been so closely adapted to their needs; this latter argument, however, was purely speculative—it could not be tested in practice.

In the late 1950s study directed at external examinations snowballed in secondary modern schools, 'directly contrary', as Joan Davis has put it, 'to the Minister's regulations and expressed policy' (Davis, 1962, 61). The College of Preceptors, the Royal Society of Arts and other bodies prepared examinations for children aged fifteen; Table II summarises this development which led finally, as a result of the recommendations of the Beloe Committee, to the Certificate of Secondary Education established in 1965.

Impressive though the rate of increase is, the extent of this development should not be exaggerated. The 55,000 pupils from modern schools sitting an external examination in 1960 represented approximately one in eight of the relevant age group in these schools (and the remaining all-age schools). Nonetheless the development remains significant. Qualifications of some kind were now more necessary for those entering on apprenticeships or skilled employment; parents were demanding them, schools found that they not only provided a clear objective for some, at least, of the older pupils but raised general morale and the status of the school in the community (Carter, 1957, 37-48). There remained, of course, wide differences between the amenities and opportunities offered by the grammar and even the best of the new modern schools. But the modern schools, by their own efforts, had succeeded in considerably blurring the sharp edges between what had been planned as distinctively different types of education.

Parental aspirations

So far as many parents were concerned the grammar school

TABLE II

Candidates from secondary modern schools
entering for external examinations

Examinations	1st Year of exam.	Type	Age	Number of Candidates					
				1955	1956	1957	1958	1959	1960
G.C.E. O Level	1951	Subject	16+	7,334	8,571	10,986	16,444	19,407	21,680
A Level						280	343	385	597
College of Preceptors School Certificate	1953	Group	15+	1,540	1,935	3,046	5,305	8,202	11,148
Royal Society of Arts School Certificate	1954	Group	16+				3,904	6,833	9,086
Lancashire and Cheshire U. of E. I. School Certificate	1956	Subject	16+				1,930	3,467	4,849
Union of Educational Institutions School Certificate	1958	Group	16+				730	1,618	3,418
Northern Counties School Certificate	1959	Group	15+					2,506	4,238
East Midland E.C. School Certificate	1960	Subject	16+						385

remained *the* secondary school at this period, eleven plus selection 'the scholarship'. This had been a longstanding pattern, which had not been fundamentally changed since the 1944 Act, so that those looking for the new opportunities promised for secondary education inevitably looked to the grammar school. Not only was it the only school leading to the universities and professions (apart from some technical schools), but also it had long been associated with entry to white-collar rather than manual employment. Parents who wanted their children to have a good education, to get on in life, were determined to get them into grammar school.

How strong this determination was can be shown from the following example. In 1954 in Nottingham, there were 447 grammar school places available but over 4,400 children aged 10. In view of the shortage of places, the junior school heads only entered for the selective examination those children thought to have some chance of passing; 1,321 children were picked on this basis. But parents could ask that their children be given a trial, and in spite of the teachers' recommendations and the length of the odds (ten to one in this case), the parents of another 1,395 children insisted that they sit for the examination. In all, then, 2,716 children competed for the 447 places and inevitably 2,269 'failed', among these, it must be supposed, most of the additional parental entries (*Education*, 27 August 1954).

An inquiry in Hertfordshire two years earlier had revealed much the same position. In this case all the parents of children aged ten to eleven were asked what kind of school they would like their sons and daughters to attend. Over half preferred the grammar school and a fifth the technical school; only 16 per cent favoured the modern school. Analysis of the replies showed that skilled workers particularly preferred the grammar school; also that the more thought parents had given to their child's education, the more marked was their preference for the grammar school, and that the majority of parents who felt this way held their opinions strongly (Glass, 1954, 160ff). Summing up the evidence, Professor T. H. Marshall commented that it revealed 'all too clearly' that 'parents who care about education and realise its influence on future careers . . . are immensely anxious to get their children into grammar schools'. There is, he concluded, 'a great deal of frustrated educational ambition' (*T.E.S.*, 20 August 1954).

It is true that many parents whose children were relegated to modern schools accepted the situation, and that parents whose children were in grammar schools were often opposed to the introduction of comprehensive education. Nonetheless the growing strength of parental pressure, referred to above, is a factor to be borne in mind when it comes to interpreting reasons for the move to comprehensive education. This had its political implications to which local party organisations in particular were sensitive. It may be noted that after the Labour Party had lost office in 1951 the comprehensive school once more figured high on the list of priorities in all statements on educational policy. The Conservative Party, as has been seen, had already made a particular point of safeguarding diversity of provision and the grammar school. It is during this decade, therefore, that the comprehensive school began to enter the realm of party politics.

Social class and educational opportunity

A new factor in the situation from the early 1950s was the increasing number of sociological surveys relating to education. These pointed to a direct relationship between social class and educational opportunity and underlined that the selective system resulted in wastage of ability.

The first study of this kind, published in 1953, was concerned to discover the effect of the 1944 Act on the social composition of children at certain grammar and modern schools; the sample consisted of 700 boys aged thirteen to fourteen in four grammar and five secondary modern schools in Greater London. Basing their analysis on a careful assessment of the social background of the pupils, the investigators found that 'the difference in social composition between the two types of school is striking. The secondary modern schools cater very largely for the sons of manual workers, especially the semi-skilled and unskilled.' By contrast this class was 'markedly under-represented' in the grammar schools investigated; in none of these did they constitute as much as a quarter of the pupils and in one only 6.9 per cent. Conversely, very few middle-class children were found in secondary modern schools. The conclusion was that 'despite the changes introduced into secondary education by the Education Act of 1944, it remains the case that a boy has a greater chance of entering a grammar school if he comes from a middle-class rather than a working-class home'. Seeking an explanation for this situation, the researchers pointed to 'the crucial role played by intelligence tests in the present selection procedure'; these, they held, favoured the middle-class child (Halsey and Gardner, 1953).

Subsequent investigations confirmed and generalised these findings. In 1954 a special report from the Central Advisory Council for Education, entitled *Early Leaving*, showed that there were wide differences in educational opportunity. In 1956 a study of the socially contrasted areas of Hertfordshire and Middlesborough, by Jean Floud and others, *Social Class and Educational Opportunity*, reached the same conclusion. Summing up the data made available in the 1950s, Taylor writes that 'the difference in social composition between the two types of school is striking. The secondary modern school caters very largely for the children of semi-skilled and unskilled manual workers, and the middle classes are under-represented' (Taylor, 1963, 51). In general it was becoming apparent that the 1944 Education Act, as interpreted in the post-war years, had not brought about any radical change in educational opportunity.

As a direct result of this kind of analysis concern now began to be expressed as to the loss or 'wastage' of ability taking place in the school system. The first comprehensive analysis of this was undertaken by the Central Advisory Council in its report entitled *15 to 18* (the Crowther Report) which was published in 1959. Volume II of this report contained the results of three substantial surveys, which provided, as Jean Floud put it, 'the most up-to-date account available of the social distribution of educational opportunity for boys in Britain, and a valuable analysis of some of the major social influences of educability'. One of these surveys, based on the result of tests administered to recruits to the Armed Forces aged between eighteen and twenty-one, divided the sample tested into six 'ability groups', and brought out strikingly the difference in opportunity between children from different social classes in the two highest ability groups, so revealing the extent of 'latent' or unused ability in the sample. It was shown, for instance, that in the second ability group, 58.6 per cent of recruits whose fathers were of the professional or managerial class had attended grammar or independent schools, compared to only 22 per cent of sons of skilled workers (of the same level of ability) and 14 per cent of sons of unskilled workers. In short, as Jean Floud summarised this material, 'the post-war movement of educational reform has brought the abler sons of skilled workers into the grammar and technical schools. However, the proportion of working-class recruits even in the highest ability groups with a selective secondary education is below that for the sons of non-manual workers; and at the second ability level, and for the sons of semi and unskilled workers in particular, it is very much lower . . . That there is a substantial reserve of uneducated ability in the offspring of working-class fathers,' she concluded, 'cannot be doubted' (Floud, 1961, pp. 66-8).

The growing critique of segregation

In all the circumstances it is not surprising that there was now a new impetus towards unifying the secondary system. In particular, the main theoretical justification for a divided system was now increasingly open to criticism; from about 1953 the theory and practice of intelligence testing, and particularly its role in selection for secondary education, began to be subjected to a radical critique (Simon, 1953; Heim, 1954). Sociologists had pointed to the influence of intelligence tests in discriminating against working-class children at eleven plus; and, as evidence accumulated, it began to be accepted that the test results inevitably reflected to some extent the child's environment. In other words it could no longer be held that they were tests of innate intelligence. This called in question not only the practice of selecting for different types of school, but also that of 'streaming' within the school. Indeed it was in the early 1950s that a few junior schools first began deliberately to abandon this process (Freeland, 1957).

It was also in the mid-1950s that discussion about the comprehensive school began to shift from the realm of speculation to that of practical experience. Though such schools remained very few, some of these—at Windermere, the Isle of Man, Anglesey and Middlesex—had been in existence from five to ten years; some estimate of their

63

viability as schools could, therefore, be made, while those teaching in these schools could now write about their experience. In 1954 Robin Pedley, then of the University of Leicester, visited many of these schools (including the 'interim' comprehensive schools in London) and summarised information and impressions in a series of articles in *Education*. These subsequently appeared in a booklet, *Comprehensive Schools Today*, together with critical comments by four well-known educationists: H. C. Dent, Harold Shearman (Chairman of the Education Committee of the L.C.C.), Eric James and W. P. Alexander—a publication that aroused very widespread interest. Studies accumulated over the next three years; in *Comprehensive Education, A New Approach* (1956), Pedley put forward the idea of a two-tier system of comprehensive education as a better solution educationally and administratively than the 11-18 school. Two collections of articles by heads and assistants teaching in comprehensive schools followed, *New Trends in English Education*, 1957, and, published by the N.U.T., *Inside the Comprehensive School*, 1958. At the same time discussion about the new schools was widespread in the educational press.

In the meantime the effects of educational segregation were being subjected to a new analysis. In 1955 a survey carried through by P. E. Vernon, covering all boys aged fourteen in Southampton, showed that the I.Q.s of pupils selected for the grammar and technical schools rose by an average of 4·9 points in three or four years, while those of pupils allocated to modern schools declined by 1·9 points. Similar but slightly greater differences were independently found in another area by J. C. Daniels. One of the main arguments in support of the view that tests measured innate intelligence had been that I.Q. scores for the same child normally did not change. Evidence that they did, and in the way described, indicated that it was not innate intelligence that was being measured and showed (as Vernon put it) that 'modern schools (together with the home environment from which modern school pupils come) provide a poorer stimulus to general intellectual development than do grammar and technical schools (and grammar school pupils' homes)' (*T.E.S.*, 6 May and 3 June, 1955). In the same year (1955) the first of a number of investigations into streaming in the junior school was completed. The investigation showed that early streaming 'reflects social class much more than it does real ability, since those quicker to read mostly come from middle-class homes' (Vernon, 1957, 43); the effects of streaming, it was concluded, 'are far-reaching and cumulative'.

It was, then, in a new situation that the British Psychological Society set up a special working party composed of most of the leading educational psychologists in the country to consider and report on *Secondary School Selection* (1957). This led to a significant modification of earlier theories as to the nature of 'intelligence', on the basis of which streaming and differentiation had been recommended by psychologists to the Hadow and Spens Committees before the war. Indeed the section of streaming refers directly to this point: 'Few nowadays would subscribe to the statement made in the Spens report: "We are informed that, with few exceptions, it is possible at a very early age to predict with some degree of accuracy, the ultimate level of a child's intellectual powers".' Intelligence, it was now held, as it manifested itself in daily life, was partly a resultant of environmental stimulation. The conclusion was that selection at the early age of ten or eleven should be superseded, since it could no longer be justified on psychological grounds, and that streaming in the junior school should be avoided (Vernon, 1957, 42-3).

This report implied the rejection of the Hadow-Spens theories of differentiation, on the basis of which the divided system of education had been developed. In the same year (1957) a large-scale investigation by the National Foundation of Educational Research—which had produced many of the tests used in selection—estimated that of every 1,000 children allocated at the age of eleven, 122 were wrongly assessed; half of these being wrongly allocated to a grammar school, half wrongly assigned to a modern school. Even if the most stringent methods of allocation were applied, it would be impossible to reduce this error below 10 per cent of the candidates; in other words, of an average year-group at that period, some 70,000 children would be sent to the 'wrong' type of school (Yates and Pidgeon, 1957, 144-5, 186).

From many different areas, therefore, information accumulated which raised doubts about the divided system —from the schools, parents, psychologists, sociologists— while at the same time some information was beginning to come to hand about the new educational perspectives of the pioneer comprehensive schools. All this contributed to that new thinking in education which the Crowther Report stressed was necessary. Nor is it surprising that this report, issued in 1959, underlined the need for a more flexible structure of secondary schooling.

The defence of the grammar school

There were many, however, who were by no means convinced by the investigations summarised above. Indeed the conflict of opinion over the organisation of secondary education sharpened, sometimes dramatically, in the mid-'50s. In 1951 Eric James followed up his earlier book with *Education for Leadership*, which again drew on Plato's philosophy to make a strong case for the grammar school —as a school specifically adapted for the education of the most able children. This book, referring to American experience, contained a sharp attack on the idea of the comprehensive school; for the 'brilliant' child, James argued, 'it would be disastrous . . . the interests of the most gifted could not be safeguarded', what was needed, on the other hand, was more 'super-selective' schools—like the Manchester Grammar School, 'overtly creaming' a large urban area. 'It is perfectly possible to recognise high general intelligence, certainly by the age of ten,' James argued; such brilliant children must be selected early and educated for their leadership role in modern society (James, 1951, 41-56).

The future of the grammar school was, accordingly, an essential aspect of the discussion on school organisation. The need to retain these as separate institutions was stressed, for instance, by Harry Rée, then headmaster of Watford grammar school in *The Essential Grammar School* (1956). Reé saw these schools as democratic rivals of the independent sector of education, giving lower middle and working class children opportunities of competing with the products of the 'public' schools. For this a selective school was necessary. 'Selection,' wrote Rée, 'has meant that the clever child has been able to work alongside children equally clever, and has therefore gained from pitting his mind against a mind of like calibre; it has also meant that he has been able to pursue his studies in an atmosphere conducive to hard learning and studious application, and where a tradition of voluntary service and willing acceptance of responsibility has been growing up over the years' (p. 83).

The idea that the traditional academic education was particularly adapted to a cultured minority—that the health and vitality of society rested in the hands of an élite—was powerfully argued by G. H. Bantock in his *Freedom and Authority in Education* (1954). This line of thought, which implied a separate education for a minority

—derived in part from T. S. Eliot (see especially his *Notes towards the Definition of Culture*, 1948) and from writings on 'mass civilisation and minority culture' by F. R. Leavis and others—remained influential and relatively unaffected by sociological, psychological and administrative considerations.

It was at this stage that associations of grammar school teachers, which in pre-war days had been among the first supporters of the single secondary school, became more openly opposed to the comprehensive school. To launch an untried new scheme on a wholesale scale is 'both unscientific and extraordinarily dangerous' ran a statement issued in 1955 by the Joint Committee of the Four Secondary Associations (headmasters, headmistresses, assistant masters, assistant mistresses). While agreeing that there should not be a rigid classification into types of school, and that experiments with new types should continue, they believed the best policy lay 'in the retention of both grammar and modern schools and their development side by side' as 'a genuinely parallel form of organisation'. The special task of the modern school was the education of children 'whose intellectual ability is only moderate'. The grammar school had 'its own peculiar responsibility', to fulfil 'the greatest national duty of educating the nation's most intellectually able children to the limit of their ability, no matter what their social or financial status may be'. It was the grammar school that carried 'the weight of . . . tradition' in English education, rendering a service 'which cannot without grave loss be diluted or dispensed with'. In a pamphlet issued in 1958, the Assistant Masters Association, while welcoming experiment in the organisation of secondary education, stressed that 'the nation should resolutely resist any developments which might destroy or damage the grammar schools' (A.M.A., 1958).

5

Comprehensive schools take root, 1953-62

Conditions for development

During the years when educational expansion was beginning to break down the rigidities of the secondary system, and it slowly became clear that this expansion must continue, the first comprehensive schools were taking firm root and their numbers added to. By 1954 there were sixteen schools. Three years later the Minister of Education, Edward (now Sir Edward) Boyle, reported that there were 32 in being, 8 under construction, 13 more approved (*Hansard* 18 July 1957).

The opening of Kidbrooke in London marked a new phase in this development. Born in a turmoil of political controversy—with petition and counter-petition circulating in the locality—this was the first purpose-built comprehensive school erected in an urban area. Not only educationists but the public generally were fascinated by this new school for girls with its six science laboratories, nine housecraft centres, five gymnasia, and 16½ acres of playing fields. The school was opened to organised parties of visitors in July and these were quickly booked to capacity. The fact that the post-war building boom was in its early stages and new secondary school building only beginning added to the novelty. 'Britain's great new palace of educational varieties . . . a blaze of colour—crimson, yellow and blue' was how the *News Chronicle* saw it. The *Manchester Guardian*, more soberly, commented that the school had had 'a more controversial beginning than can have been experienced by any other educational project'. The suggested purchase of a £3,000 statue (which the *Daily Sketch* called 'a £3,000 insult'), an unofficial bus strike caused by coping with the number of girls to be transported, visits of eminent people to the school, the cost of repairs and other events kept Kidbrooke's name in the news for months.

The novelty wore off comparatively soon for by 1957 the L.C.C. had opened eleven fully comprehensive schools (five based on former grammar schools) and five 'county complements'. Meanwhile two Coventry schools (Caludon Castle and Woodlands) had started in 1954, and two at Birmingham (Sheldon Heath and Great Barr) in 1955 and 1956. Other new schools were for the most part in the countryside, in the three Yorkshire Ridings, the Welsh counties and elsewhere.

These developments could not fail to strengthen the movement for comprehensive education but, as Pedley put it at the time, 'as powerful local authorities like London, the West Riding, Staffordshire, Swansea and Manchester have pressed on with their plans for comprehensive schools, so the opposition of the Ministry has hardened' (Pedley, 1956, 109). In 1953 Miss Horsbrugh had refused to allow the L.C.C. to incorporate Eltham Hill Girls High School in Kidbrooke; later that year she refused to allow the same authority to expand the Bec Grammar School as a comprehensive school. Her successor, Sir David Eccles, shortly after taking office late in 1954, took an early opportunity to reassure grammar school teachers as to his intentions. In setting the pattern of secondary education, he said, 'one must choose between justice and equality, for it is impossible to apply both principles at once. Those who support comprehensive schools prefer equality. Her Majesty's present government prefer justice. My colleagues and I will never agree to the assassination of the grammar schools' (*The Schoolmaster*, 7 January 1955).

By 'assassination' Sir David Eccles, as he explained, meant the absorption of grammar schools into comprehensive units. Since grammar schools existed in most areas of the country, this condition (except where exceptions were made) confined the development of comprehensive schools almost entirely to new housing estates. In general terms this in fact was the policy pursued during these years; comprehensive school experiments, announced the Minister in 1955, would only be approved if they did not compete with any existing school, adding the proviso that they must contain over 2,000 pupils each (in order to 'throw up' a viable sixth form) (*The Schoolmaster*, 22 August 1955).

This was a time, as has been noted, when there were new pressures on the schools from many angles and a speeding up of the programme of school building appeared as a very present need. The government's intentions were clearly expressed in a White Paper published in December 1958, *Secondary Education for All, a New Drive*. This put the emphasis on the development of advanced courses in secondary modern schools and restated the government's determination to maintain the grammar schools as separate entities. 'Experiments' with comprehensive schools would not be ruled out if proposed on 'genuine educational grounds'. They could, however, only be permitted in country districts with sparse populations and in new housing estates where there were no existing schools whatever —grammar, technical or modern. The extension of a grammar school to become comprehensive was here defined as 'bringing to an end an existing grammar school . . . simply in order that a new comprehensive school

71

may enjoy a monopoly of the abler children within its area', and as 'completely abolishing' parents' freedom of choice. 'A downright militant political document,' wrote the *Economist* of this policy statement, adding a demand that the Minister look again at those Labour controlled local authorities (Newport, Derbyshire, West Riding, etc.) which had announced plans to use 'the steamroller of comprehensivation'; development of the secondary modern schools, said *The Times*, means that 'the grammar school is safe'. Of the teachers' organisations it was the Joint Four which gave the White Paper the most enthusiastic welcome.

Government and local authorities

Quite a number of county authorities were, at this time, moving towards the idea of providing single secondary schools in rural areas, as had, indeed, been done since 1945 with the establishment of bilateral schools. But it was predominantly Labour controlled authorities which planned to establish fully comprehensive schools, as a step towards a comprehensive system, so that conflicts between the central authority and local authorities now almost invariably carried political overtones. Traditionally, the development of the educational service in Britain has been carried through by a 'partnership' between local and central authorities, but both the 1918 and the 1944 Acts had strengthened the power of the central authority. All plans for development by a city or county had to be 'approved' by the Ministry of Education, so that, in cases of conflict, as in the case of Kidbrooke, local authorities showed themselves highly sensitive. The Ministry itself had to bear this factor in mind in making its decisions, since the government, in its turn, was sensitive to public opinion.

Nevertheless the mid-1950s were marked by a series of

conflicts between local authorities, wishing to establish comprehensive schools, and the Ministry, wishing to prevent this development except on its own terms. Immediately after Sir David Eccles took office a number of clashes took place of which the most important were those with Manchester and Swansea. In Manchester the local authority wished to transform existing school accommodation at Wythenshawe (involving five schools) as three comprehensive schools and to open them to a non-selective entry in September that year (1955). The plan was put to the Ministry in April and all the necessary arrangements made to go ahead. Four days before the beginning of the school term the plan was rejected by the Minister on the grounds that the units proposed fail 'to provide the conditions in which the merits of this comparatively untried type of school can be properly tested' and that it involved 'an uneconomic use of expensive resources'. It might be a long time before Manchester and the Ministry saw eye to eye again, commented the *Manchester Guardian*; no doubt there was much to be said on both sides but 'one cannot think that the Minister's method of handling the question contributes much to a reasonable settlement'.

Later that year the Minister rejected a proposal that the four secondary schools in Swansea should eventually be merged into 'multilateral' schools. He could not agree, he told a deputation from the authority 'to the extinction of the existing grammar schools, whose traditions were too good and too precious to be endangered'. Two of the proposed schools, however, could be established on new housing estates (*T.E.S.*, 6 January 1956). It is worth recalling that Swansea had proposed a complete system of multilateral schools in its post-war development plan, and this had been approved, in principle, by the Minister of Education in 1949. The authority wished, now, to implement this plan.

In practice, in urban areas, only schools on new housing estates could be developed in the 1950s. The post-war plans of other authorities, for instance Oldham and Bradford, and several others, could not be implemented in accordance with the conditions laid down in 1955 and reinforced later. These conditions inevitably led to a 'freezing' of the official system which had Ministerial support. Action in later years against other authorities reinforced this position. In 1958 the county borough of Newport, in Monmouthshire, proposed to replace the city's twelve modern, one technical and four grammar schools by four comprehensive schools, with the aim of abolishing selection throughout the city by 1960. This plan was rejected by the Minister. The Education Committee, in reply, reaffirmed their intention 'in keeping with their powers, to move towards abolition of the eleven plus and the segregation of pupils and to establish the full comprehensive system as and when opportunity offers' (*Education*, 12 September 1958). Early in 1959 Geoffrey Lloyd, who had succeeded Sir David Eccles as Minister for Education, appeared to be pursuing the same policy when he rejected a proposal by Darlington to establish a comprehensive school.

The new comprehensive schools—academic organisation

What was going on at this time within the comprehensive schools that had begun work? As has been seen, these varied widely, from the single school in a rural area to complete systems on two islands, from new schools isolated on completely new housing estates to the considerable nucleus of schools established in London and Coventry.

Two strands can be distinguished in the pre-history and early history of the comprehensive school. The original conception had been that the single secondary school

74

should be a 'multilateral' school, providing all the various courses of study needed at the secondary stage. This had been overlaid, after the clearer development of different types of school (grammar, technical and modern), by the concept of a common school comprising different types of education, though, inherent in all thinking about the common school, had been belief in providing a common core of education so far as possible. On the other hand the growing rigidity of the divided system, and the intensification of streaming within schools, operated in another direction—to suggest that children were best provided for by a very precise system of classification. In practice, streaming corresponded to the need to prepare children for highly competitive examinations at the end of the primary course, at fifteen or sixteen, and at the stage of university entry. One thing was clear, if in the prevailing critical atmosphere in which they were regarded as strictly experimental, comprehensive schools were to prove themselves, then they must register success on the grammar school footrule of the external examination. By contrast, there were no blueprints for a common school, with an integrated curriculum.

In all the circumstances it is not surprising to find that the earliest comprehensive schools, many of which developed around the nucleus of a grammar school, primarily stressed academic attainment and introduced streaming. But, from the outset, they saw this not as a permanent classification so much as a means of educational guidance within the context of an all-inclusive school.

The headmaster of Holyhead school, describing its organisation in 1956, stressed particularly the Hadow principle of 'progressive differentiation'. In other words, streaming and setting were used in an attempt to ensure that each pupil worked at the pace suitable to him. 'Progressive differentiation during the first four years,' wrote the headmaster, 'leads the pupil into that "stream" of co-ordinated activities for which he has discovered a marked aptitude.' There was 'preliminary segregation' during the first year (a form of 'diagnosis' replacing the superseded eleven plus) but it did not reach finality until the end of four years. Efficient setting of this kind 'completely refutes the popular accusation of retarding the bright and forcing the slow' (*T.E.S.*, 27 January 1956).

In fact, the chief critic of the comprehensive school, Eric James, had recently been reported as suggesting that such schools lacked organisation and standards, that the children were 'ungraded, untested and unperturbed' (*The Schoolmaster*, 30 April 1954). The truth, responded Robin Pedley, summing up the practice of a number of schools, 'is exactly opposite . . . the whole structure of today's schools of comprehensive type is based on differentiation of courses and classes'. He added that this ran counter to the ideas of some advocates of the comprehensive school (Pedley, 1955, 2, 3).

In London, where comprehensive reorganisation was only partial, there was still an eleven plus examination. When Kidbrooke school opened in 1954, the children admitted were divided into thirteen streams on the basis of marks in the selection examination. But to stress the extent of differentiation at this stage would be to give a wrong emphasis. What may be called the 'second wave' of London schools set out to provide a general course, common to all pupils, for the first three years, despite the retention of forms of streaming. 'The curriculum is a common one for all the forms', it was reported in the survey of London schools published by the L.C.C. in 1961, though there were minor differences as between schools. There had been little doubt that it was desirable to provide 'a broadly based general course for the whole of the first three years' (L.C.C., 1961, 34). In London, of course, there had been opposition in principle to the tripartite system and much thought had been given to the development of a common secondary school. An early advisory booklet issued by the L.C.C. had suggested 'that the schools should be organised as unified wholes, and not in clearly defined sides corresponding to grammar, technical and modern schools' (L.C.C., 1953, 7).

To establish a common course, even for the first three years, was a new venture. In the large subject departments of the new London schools a great deal of thought was given to evolving syllabuses, which, if treated at different levels, could be effectively taught to all the pupils. The content of syllabuses on history, English, science, mathematics, languages, geography and other subjects was restructured as a result of this re-thinking and of the experience gained in teaching. 'Until September 1955,' wrote three members of the English department at Holloway School in London, which opened at that time, 'the authors of this article were teaching in a grammar school, a secondary modern school and a special school for backward children. Specialist interests covered the library, speech training, drama and visual arts. Nevertheless we had felt the inadequacies of the tripartite system and looked to the comprehensive school for a remedy. We found common ground in ideas and ideals. All three of us were form-masters of boys in the new comprehensive first year and our discussions quickly led us to consider a common syllabus.' Was this possible? The department concluded that it was, and that to evolve such a syllabus was of 'the utmost importance if the comprehensive idea is to succeed', since only by this means were the old barriers to be overcome, and pupils 'to enjoy the same opportunities' (Brown, *et al.*, 1957, 159-66).

Nonetheless the common course was usually defined in such a way as to allow for treatment at different levels, since streaming was still in operation. In the mid-fifties, however, there were moves to modify classification on these lines. Some schools adopted the system of 'bands', that is, divided pupils into three main ability groupings each consisting of three, four or five classes which were unstreamed within that band. Other schools (Woodberry Down in London and Caludon Castle at Coventry are examples) formed non-streamed, or 'mixed ability', classes for such subjects as music, physical education and crafts, and used a system of setting for mathematics, science and languages. The various forms of internal organisation in London in the 1950s are well set out in the survey *London Comprehensive Schools* covering sixteen varying schools (L.C.C., 1961, 31 ff.). This publication reflects a view then accepted as axiomatic: 'none of the schools bases its organisation upon the impracticable assumption that teaching groups covering the whole range of ability are suitable or desirable' (p. 32).

There is a good deal of evidence to show that, however schools were organised, transfer between streams was relatively easy and that children from lower streams, who developed the ability and interest in continuing study, could move into the fifth and sixth forms. The headmaster of Wandsworth School, London, one which had developed from a grammar school in 1956, summarised its experience some years later. Of 410 boys aged eleven who entered the school in September 1956—without any selection—130 entered the sixth form in September 1961. 'Boys from every one of the fourteen forms of 1956 entrants reached the sixth, and from nine of these fourteen forms the academic sixth. Of the original 410 entrants only 62 had the I.Q. of 115 or over that distinguishes the "grammar category"' (King, 1962, 15).

In general, after completion of the three year common course, schools provided a variety of courses to choose from. In the London schools these included technical, craft and commercial courses of various kinds in parallel with an 'academic' course; in effect, a multilateral form of organisation. Since the choice made for the fourth year is clearly of great importance to each individual pupil, various systems of 'guidance' or 'counselling' were introduced, involving teacher and youth employment officer, parent and child. As courses became established more pupils stayed on beyond the leaving age and there began to develop what became known as 'the new sixth form'. In other words, it was not only pupils staying on to take 'A' level G.C.E. who made up sixth forms but others following secretarial, pre-nursing, or other courses and taking 'O' level subjects at seventeen (L.C.C., 1961, 58-9). In general, more varied sixth forms were developing than those in the traditional grammar schools.

Most of the new purpose-built comprehensive schools in urban areas were, of course, large schools—as it had been laid down that they must be. This had its advantages from the point of view of providing variety of choice, particularly at sixth form level. A school of 1,600 pupils had a teaching staff of about 80. This implied strong departments covering the main subjects which could act as nuclei for discussion of the content and methods of education. There might, for instance, be several specialist art teachers and art rooms comprising a wide range of equipment, talent and experience. In addition, the large school could be provided with a swimming bath and other particular amenities. That comprehensive schools were so large had been the subject of much adverse criticism; it was soon realised that, in certain respects, it could be an advantage.

The new comprehensive schools—social organisation

Some of the early comprehensive schools, established in

areas where there was no effective alternative, had less than 1,000 pupils. The smallest, as has been noted, was Windermere with 200, taking in all the boys in its area. Some in Staffordshire were planned for 900. In Anglesey, there were 1,000 at Holyhead, at Douglas in the Isle of Man, slightly more. But the new urban schools built in the 1950s ranged from about 1,200 to a maximum of 2,200, with an average of about 1,600. This kind of size had been insisted upon, it may be remembered, as early as 1947 when the Ministry laid down that a single secondary school could only be a viable unit if the annual entry was not less than 300 or 330. This calculation was based not only on assumptions about the proportion of different types of mind among an age-group of children, but also on the belief that no more children would remain on beyond the statutory leaving age than had been common before the war. On these grounds it was argued that only a comprehensive school of 1,600 could produce a sixth form of adequate size. As a result, when many children besides those in the 'academic' streams began to stay on, comprehensive schools tended further to increase in size.

There were, however, other reasons for building large schools in urban areas. London, where sites were extremely short and expensive and the population dense, had to think in these terms; from the days of the School Board large schools, housing over 1,000 children, had been traditional. Coventry had earmarked a group of sites on the outskirts of the city, some of which extended to 60 acres. Here also the large school, with the many amenities this could imply, seemed appropriate. It was, however, recognised that the large comprehensive school would require special forms of organisation enabling individual children to be well known by a group of teachers, and providing each with a base in the school where he could feel he belonged.

Broadly speaking, three different solutions were found, though elements of each were sometimes combined.

The year group was the main form of organisation adopted by the first London schools, for instance, Mayfield and Parliament Hill, both girls' schools. Each class has its form mistress but there is also a year mistress who may have thirteen or fourteen forms in her unit covering the whole year group. Class teachers and the year mistress work together and a number of activities are arranged for the year as a whole. In some instances both class teachers and year teacher move with their age-group up the school so that the relationships established with both pupils and parents persist.

The Coventry schools from the first, however, were planned on a different principle. Both at Woodlands and Caludon Castle, the two first schools, a physical house system formed part of the school buildings. Each house comprises about 150 pupils under a housemaster and at least five members of staff; its accommodation comprises an assembly room, used also as dining hall, a quiet room, staffroom and housemaster's room. Caludon Castle, to take a concrete example, has 1,500 boys in ten houses. Four of these are set aside for pupils aged eleven to thirteen, as a means of easing young children into the secondary stage. Towards the end of the second year each child is allocated to one of the six senior houses, in such a way as to ensure a mixed ability entry to each house. Every teacher attached to a house is allotted a 'tutor-group' covering all age-groups and abilities. The housemaster himself, with the aid of his staff, aims to know all the children in his house, their records and problems, and often knows most of the parents. Besides providing for close contact between teachers and pupils, this form of organisation was intended to enable pupils to exercise responsibilities within the house structure (Firth, 1963, 111-30). A similar kind of house system was later adopted in some London schools, at West Bromwich, Hull and elsewhere; other comprehensive schools have introduced it in a modified form since buildings were not originally planned on this pattern.

A horizontal division into lower, middle and upper school is the third pattern, first developed at Sheldon Heath in Birmingham, a comprehensive school designed for 2,200 pupils which opened in 1955. Here three separate buildings were erected on the same site, a lower, a middle and an upper school. The idea of forming a special 'lower school', or department, for children of eleven to thirteen, had already been strongly recommended, for instance in the Norwood report—and was particularly apt when two schools were amalgamated to make a single comprehensive school. At Holyhead, where this was the case, a junior department under its own head had been formed. But Sheldon Heath was the first school to be purpose-built on this principle, and here each of the three departments, or 'schools', had its own head under the aegis of the headmaster. In this case teachers are attached to lower, middle or upper school, although this does not prevent teaching across the age range. This system, it has been suggested, is well adapted to provide differing treatment for various age levels; the upper school, for instance, can be allowed considerable freedom as a separate unit. It is interesting to note that, as a result of this form of organisation, Sheldon Heath has found no need for the prefect system (Smith, 1958, 88-94).

As additional schools have become established, new methods have been evolved as a variation of these three main forms of organisation. For instance there has been a combination, or fusion, of the house (or 'vertical') system with the year-group ('horizontal') system. In each case the overriding aim is the same, that of ensuring that each individual child is known and cared for within the large school—and not only so far as his intellectual development is concerned but also his general development. To solve the practical problems of organising large schools has been also, in a very real sense, to enhance the particular contribution the comprehensive school can make to the education of the whole child.

The Leicestershire Experiment—a two-tier system

A new phase in the development of comprehensive schools was heralded when, in 1957, the Leicestershire County Council decided to experiment with a 'two-tier' system in two areas of the county. There has already been a breaking down of the large comprehensive school into horizontal units, and, as early as 1956, it had been suggested that there was much to be said for organising such schools in two distinct tiers with a break at fifteen or sixteen (Pedley, 1956). Now, with increasing popular concern about the operation of selection and gathering evidence of the weaknesses of the tests used, local authorities were beginning to think again about the programmes they had adopted in the early post-war years. As the Director of Education for Leicestershire wrote, he had once accepted without demur the tripartite system 'backed as it was by the Norwood Report and by the Ministry of Education's pamphlet *The New Secondary Education*' but it was now clear that the practice of selection was no longer tenable. With 'public disapprobation of the bi-partite system' continuing to gain momentum', local authorities, he concluded, 'will be relentlessly driven to adopt the large scale comprehensive school' unless some satisfactory alternative was devised (Mason, *The Leicestershire Experiment (and Plan)*, 1960 ed., 9, 13).

The alternative which was accepted, and which it was decided to act upon in a limited area forthwith, involved adaptation of the existing system. One of the main points in its favour was that it would require hardly any new building. The plan was to transform the secondary modern schools into comprehensive 'high' schools, taking in all the local children at the age of eleven, and to turn the grammar schools (under the same name) into upper schools taking in children at fourteen. When children reached the age of fourteen, parents were to be offered a choice. Either they could opt for the grammar (upper) school, with the assurance that their child would be allotted a place, or the child could remain in the 'high' school until the leaving age. There was a proviso that in opting for the upper school parents must guarantee to keep their child in school for at least two years, until the age of sixteen.

This straightforward scheme did not involve the closure of any existing school, nor the building of any completely new school, and did not, in practice, require the permission of the Minister. It was advanced by a county authority which was certainly not Labour controlled, but which was voicing doubts now felt by many. In addition, the plans were regarded in the first place as purely experimental, to be tried on a limited scale. These two points were underlined by Sir Edward Boyle, Parliamentary Secretary to the Ministry, when he publicly welcomed the scheme (*T.E.S.*, 10 May 1957).

The Leicestershire Plan, as it soon became known, initially aroused some criticism from supporters of comprehensive schools on the grounds that some fourteen year olds (on the basis of their parents' choice) would be left behind in the 'high' schools in something of a dead end. But in 1966 the authority decided (in the light of nearly a decade of experience) that, when the leaving age was raised to sixteen, all children would automatically go on to the upper schools—so creating a genuinely end-on system. A major advantage of the scheme was that it was possible to eliminate the selection examination in the experimental areas within three years. These districts of Leicestershire were the first in England where the eleven plus ceased to operate. In 1960 the scheme, adjudged a success, was extended to three other areas in the county, and since then has gradually come into operation in the county as a whole. Many deputations from other authorities visited the Leicestershire schools in the early years, examining with interest the workings of this plan.

A decade of experience—the position in 1962

In spite of the difficulties, both in terms of resources allocated for new school buildings and of official policy, the number of comprehensive schools increased in the late 1950s and early 1960s. In January 1962 the Ministry of Education gave the number of comprehensive schools as 152. If to these were added schools classified by the Ministry as 'bilateral and multilateral' and 'other secondary' the total of comprehensive or near-comprehensive schools would, of course, be greater. These categories, taken together, now provided for approximately one in ten of secondary school pupils (*Education in 1962*, 120).

London remained firmly in the lead with 53.4 per cent of the relevant age groups in fifty-eight schools. Outside the capital, Coventry had been joined as a centre of development by Bristol which, taking advantage of permission to build on new housing estates, had a ring of new comprehensive schools surrounding the city. Schools of this type had also been established in some of the new towns which provided a fruitful ground for their development, for instance Crawley in Sussex, Harlow in Essex, and Kirkby in Lancashire, and these exercised an influence on the surrounding counties. Among the greater industrial cities of the midlands and north with one or more such schools were

Birmingham, Leeds, Manchester, Nottingham, Sheffield. But it must be noted that few of these urban schools were fully comprehensive since they were often single units within a predominantly selective system; in general, therefore, their intake consisted of pupils who had not won a place in a grammar school. This was also true of London (where direct grant schools and voluntary aided grammar schools remained in considerable numbers), and of Coventry where there were two direct grant boys' schools as well as two maintained girls' grammar schools. There were, however, signs that some parents were ready to opt for a comprehensive school even if their child gained a grammar school place.

That grammar schools continued to attract the most advanced children—or those whose attainment at eleven plus was above average—meant that the larger comprehensive schools, with the greatest opportunities of experimenting with new methods, did not have a representative intake. The only genuinely comprehensive schools in this sense, taking nearly all local children of secondary school age, were in county areas, chiefly the North and West Ridings of Yorkshire, midland counties such as Staffordshire and now Leicestershire, Westmorland, and, more recently, counties in the south-west. In Wales, however, there had been considerable advances and bilateral schools were common in most counties. Welsh grammar schools traditionally took in a much higher proportion of each age group than the English; in Merioneth, for instance, over 60 per cent of children gained grammar school places. As a result the Welsh schools, though called bilateral, usually had a fluid form of organisation rather than clearly defined 'sides' and were really indistinguishable from comprehensive schools; nor, were these schools creamed.

While, therefore, Anglesey remained the only Welsh

authority to abolish the eleven plus examination, there were, by 1961, twenty-two comprehensive schools in other Welsh counties—nearly all the secondary schools of Merioneth, and Montgomery, Cardiganshire and Caernarvonshire, several in Pembrokeshire, and a fine new school in Glamorgan (Aberavon). In the county boroughs progress was slower, but by 1961 Newport had succeeded in establishing two of its comprehensive schools while Swansea, by breaking down inner divisions, had transformed its two multilateral schools into comprehensive schools.

In Scotland, also, there had been new moves. Glasgow opened its first two comprehensive schools in 1954, marking a change of policy in urban areas where there had always been more differentiation of schools than in the countryside. By 1962 Glasgow had twenty-two comprehensive schools of two types; some were four-year schools, some six-year, those in the former who wished to continue their education being able to transfer to the six-year school (*Forum*, 1962, Vol. 5, No. 1).

The actual number of comprehensive schools was still relatively small. But the significant factor—as those responsible for both central and local administration were now aware—was not so much the number of schools that had been established as the example that had been set, at a time when it was becoming more and more difficult to maintain confidence in the process of selection. In particular, the success of the Leicestershire Plan provided a new perspective. Other authorities now began to think in terms not merely of establishing the occasional comprehensive school, within the limitations still officially laid down, but of reorganising their whole provision for secondary education on fully comprehensive lines.

6

Towards a comprehensive system of secondary education

A quarter of all local education authorities made major changes in their selection procedures between 1960 and 1964. This was the conclusion of a survey undertaken by the National Foundation for Educational Research which provided evidence of growing disquiet. There was, equally, evidence of a new readiness to accept the comprehensive solution; in 1964 71 per cent of all authorities either had, or intended to establish, some form of comprehensive education. Commenting on these findings, the Foundation —a body in close contact with local authorities—concluded that an end to selection at eleven 'is at least possible' (N.F.E.R., 1964).

It was, of course, local administrators who bore the brunt of parental objections to selection, and the onus of administering tests now known to be inadequate for their purpose. Recognition that planning since 1945, under official guidance from the Ministry, had taken a mistaken direction encouraged an independent approach to the problems of school organisation. To look afresh in the early 1960s at the problems involved in eleven plus selection was to see matters in a new light. The Chief Education Officer for Lancashire now described the examination as an 'archaic monstrosity'.

Moreover, it could no longer be argued that the comprehensive school was an untried experiment. Many authorities, which had established one or two schools, had been watching these with interest. A considerable number had been operating for over ten years and had registered remarkable success, not only in the traditional terms of examination results but also in their evident ability to retain children at school after the leaving age (Eggleston, 1967). This was now a question of increasing interest since it was known that the raising of the school leaving age was probable. This, of course, would involve the adaptation of buildings and provision of additional places—and here was another reason for thinking ahead and deciding now how that provision should be made. Then, in 1964, the kind of arguments earlier advanced in the Crowther report (1959) —about the need for a higher general level of education, the wastage of ability and social discrimination—were strongly reinforced with publication of the Robbins report on higher education accompanied by volumes of evidence including much special research.

These were some of the main factors contributing to what may be called a new grass roots movement to reorganise secondary education on comprehensive lines, a movement crowned in 1965 by the decision of a new Labour government to make this national policy. Thereafter the former position, whereby local authorities desiring comprehensive reorganisation had been impeded from above, was reversed. It was now the Ministry which, exercising its powers of control and direction in pursuance of a comprehensive policy, took the lead in promoting change and criticised or rejected the plans of local authorities which still wished to retain selection in open or concealed form.

A grass roots movement for comprehensive reorganisation

In the spring and summer of 1963 several powerful local

89

authorities, particularly in the industrial north, clearly expressed their desire for an overall change in secondary organisation. In July, for instance, Manchester City Council resolved:

> That in order to make an end of eleven plus selection and the practice of segregating secondary pupils in this city into Grammar, Technical High and Secondary Modern Schools, the Education Committee shall prepare and present to the Council within six months proposals for converting all county secondary schools, and such other appropriate schools as may wish to participate, into comprehensive schools. It is envisaged that the new pattern of secondary education in the city will be one in which suitable schools will offer comprehensive education for pupils between the ages of eleven and eighteen without a break, while other schools will be reorganised as Junior and Senior comprehensive schools, with such other variations in the general pattern as may seem desirable: provided always that the principles of comprehensiveness and common secondary schooling are maintained. In preparing their report the Education Committee shall have discussions with the voluntary bodies and the teachers. The Council are also conscious of the need for speed and hope that it will be possible to abolish the practice of selection by 1965 (*Forum*, Vol. 6, No. 1).

It was to take two years longer for all the obstacles to be overcome, but in September 1967 the first group of eleven year olds entered the Manchester secondary schools without any form of academic selection. It was also in 1963 that Liverpool Education Committee announced its intention to work out practical plans for a transition to comprehensive reorganisation throughout the city, on lines first decided upon in 1955.

In July 1964, Lancashire Education Committee—responsible for a population of three million—resolved to introduce a comprehensive system, leaving the choice of methods open for discussion by each of the 29 divisional executive committees responsible for local areas. By this time ten other county boroughs in the geographical county were discussing or implementing plans; these included Preston, Rochdale, Blackburn, St. Helens, Bolton, Wigan and Oldham—the latter's original development plan for comprehensive schools having been held up as a result of poor allocations for new building.

In Yorkshire, where the West Riding had pioneered comprehensive education, there was a similar swing in the major county boroughs. In 1962 Sheffield City Council decided (to quote from an official memorandum) 'to move as quickly as possible towards a more comprehensive system of secondary education with the aim of abolishing segregation at eleven plus', and thereafter planned developments accordingly. Bradford City Council resolved in October 1963 to end all selection at eleven plus and at the same time authorised reorganisation of the schools to make this possible. The plan involved a two-tier system, operating initially in existing buildings and involving parental choice at thirteen, with a transition by stages to a fully comprehensive system. This move was approved by the Minister of Education, Sir Edward Boyle, who waived a statutory requirement to facilitate the transition. Accordingly, in September 1964, Bradford became the first English city to abolish selection at eleven. Among other Yorkshire cities Leeds and Hull were working out schemes, so that there was a general move towards reorganisation in the north. By now it had been recognised that fundamental changes must come (*Forum* 1965, Vol. 6, No. 3; 1966, Vol. 7, No. 2).

In the midlands, Staffordshire which had three of the earliest comprehensive schools, was developing more, the Leicestershire Plan was spreading through that county, while Derbyshire had worked out a scheme covering the county as a whole. All this was brought to national attention when a summary picture was published in the *Sunday Times* in the summer of 1964. The N.U.T. also issued a survey of changes under way which it subsequently had difficulty in keeping up to date.

As attention began to turn to the problems of a planned, and systematic, transition to a comprehensive form of organisation, considerable interest was shown in the example of Sweden, where this course had been taken— after careful and extensive research—during the 1950s and 1960s. Methods of school organisation in the United States also aroused a new interest, the city of Stoke-on-Trent being one which sent a deputation of inquiry. There were also deputations to find out about education in the U.S.S.R., where a system of common schools up to the age of fifteen was the rule. One of these consisted of members of the Committee on Higher Education (the Robbins Committee) which, reporting in October 1963, proposed a great expansion in higher education and completely rejected the notion that the 'pool of ability' was strictly limited; these findings had, of course, direct implications for the secondary stage.

The mass of statistical material in the volumes of the Robbins report provided additional evidence of the wastage of ability under the selective system. Earlier findings related to social class and educational opportunity were also reinforced by the first publication of a research unit of the Medical Research Council, under the direction of J. W. B. Douglas, *The Home and the School* (1964). In particular this survey suggested that streaming and selection operated to discriminate against working-class children by comparison with those of the middle class. If all children aged eight of a given level of measured ability had the same chance of a grammar school place as did children of the upper middle class, grammar school places would have to be increased by over fifty per cent. 'Educationally desirable qualities are hardly likely to be inborn and limited to the middle classes,' Douglas commented, 'and if we are to make full use of the potential talent of the nation's children, they should be fostered in all social classes' (Douglas, 1964, 46-9, 118-23).

It began to seem, at least to those who followed the subject closely, that all the pointers were in one direction—away from the long advocated road of diversity by means of broad divisions into separate types of school, and towards unification of the administrative system allowing for a genuine diversity within the single school. But, in practice, it was mainly authorities in the most populous areas which decided on and announced a reversal of policy. In many areas of the country selection for different types of school continued, whatever the national trend.

A change in national policy: Circular 10/65

When, in October 1964, a Labour government was elected to office, it was returned on a programme which included a promise to introduce comprehensive education. The following January, in an important debate in the House of Commons, the intentions of the government were outlined by Michael Stewart, the new Secretary of State for Education and Science (a title deriving from changes introduced in April 1964 when the former Ministry had been transformed into a Department for Education and Science). Deploring the 'separatist' system of secondary education, and pointing to its deficiencies, he drew attention to the many authorities now considering, drawing up or operating new plans; taken as a whole these were responsible for 74 per cent of children of school age in England and Wales. It was his intention to issue a Circular asking all authorities to take this course and submit plans for the reorganisation of secondary schools in their areas on comprehensive lines.

This was due warning that the central authority no longer held to the policy of retaining the grammar school as a separate institution. Plans for reorganisation affecting particular grammar schools had already aroused protest in some places; now there were more, on occasion reaching considerable dimensions. While there had been much objection to selection at eleven as it affected the majority of children, this had been the operative system and parents could do little to counter official arguments that selection was fair and right; only over a long period did criticism and protest gather a weight that could no longer be ignored. When it came to the turn of those whose children had profited from the selective system, and who believed in maintaining the grammar school as a separate institution, protests were much more organised and vocal. Governors, associations of old pupils, parents' associations, associations confined to grammar school heads and teachers, were often involved in the defence of particular schools. Liverpool, Bristol, Luton, were among places where signatures were sought for petitions, and even protest marches organised. The hard fact remained that to retain the grammar school meant retention of selection. It was this that eventually carried most weight, despite considerable support for sectional objections. As it turned out, no political party wished to become known on a national basis as the party supporting the eleven plus.

In July 1965, the promised Circular (10/65) was issued to local authorities. This declared the government's intention 'to end selection at eleven plus and to eliminate separatism in secondary education'. Local authorities were asked to submit, within a year, plans for reorganisation on comprehensive lines. The Circular was issued by

Anthony Crosland, now Secretary of State, and a similar circular went out from the Scottish office in October (Circular 600). No single pattern of organisation was, however, laid down. Instead the various patterns that had come into being or were under discussion were outlined, six in all though two of these were regarded as providing an interim solution only. The most favoured type was the 'all-through' school as established in London, Coventry and elsewhere and it was now clearly stated that such schools could freely be planned for 900 pupils and upwards.

The two patterns regarded as acceptable only for a transitional period incorporated parallel schools for pupils over the age of thirteen or fourteen and so the continuance of some form of selection. The four patterns accepted as fully comprehensive were:

1. The single-tier school for children aged 11-18.
2. A two-tier system in which all children transferred automatically at 13 or 14 to the same upper school; i.e. an 'end-on' system.
3. A two-tier system comprising schools for the 11-16 age range and sixth form colleges for those aged 16 to 18. (Only 'a limited number of experiments' on this pattern would be permitted.)
4. A two-tier system comprising a 'middle school' for children aged 8 to 12 (or 9 to 13) followed by an upper school for the age range up to 18. (Again, only 'a very small number' of this system would be allowed.)

This last pattern draws attention to the fact that one provision of the 1944 Act had been rescinded by an amending Act passed in the summer of 1964. This removed the statutory requirement that children should proceed from primary to secondary education at the age of eleven, so giving scope for more flexibility in organisation. The West Riding Education Committee had first proposed breaking

down progress from primary through secondary education in a new way, by providing a primary school to the
age of nine, then a middle school to thirteen, followed
by an upper school.

A later Circular (10/66) announced conditions relating
to finance for new school buildings. It made clear that no
funds would be forthcoming for projects which did not
accord with the transition to a comprehensive secondary
system. It was also stated at this time that funds for
educational developments would be severely limited on
account of a new balance of payments crisis. Reorganisation would have to be carried through without the allocation of any extra resources, over and above the normal
allowances where new buildings were necessary owing to
population expansion and additional places needed when
the leaving age was raised. This was clearly a severely
restrictive factor.

Local authorities now completed plans in hand, or turned
to producing schemes, though a few expressed unwilling-
ness to do so. To some extent the issues continued to be
clouded by local political controversy and confused by
changes in the control of local councils. Some educationists
still held, as had long been argued, that the move to comprehensive secondary education was inspired by a wish
to promote social equality—a 'sentimental egalitarianism'
—rather than representing a positive educational policy.
In response the general move in the direction of unifying
secondary education in many European countries was
pointed to and the fact that the technological revolution
created new educational needs and opportunities. The high
degree of specialisation hitherto accepted at the secondary
stage had been harmful and was no longer called for;
rather the need was for a broad general education for all
—which could best be provided in comprehensive schools.
These had in fact made a relevant educational contribu-

tion, by fostering both intellectual achievement and the general development of children of varied interests and abilities.

Inside the comprehensive schools—moves towards integration

Commenting on the operation of the Leicestershire Plan in 1960 the director of education for the county drew attention to its effect not only on the schools directly concerned but on junior schools. These had taken on a new life with removal of the selection examination, and were branching out in quite new directions, in the teaching of the 'new mathematics', French, art and music; a richer variety of activities was possible now that the formal teaching required for the eleven plus tests was no longer essential (Mason, 1960, 34-5). Just as the selective system of secondary schools had operated to stratify the primary school, so the ending of selection initiated a trend towards more flexible forms of organisation. In Leicestershire and to some extent in London and elsewhere, junior schools began to abolish streaming and to encourage group and individual work to a greater extent than had been possible earlier. That streaming at an early age is undesirable had been suggested at intervals since 1953, and the point was underlined by Vernon (1957), Douglas (1964) and others. With the fading of the influence of intelligence testing, and so of the conception that abilities are fixed and unchangeable, the whole emphasis began to shift from teaching homogeneous classes towards seeking new ways of facilitating active learning by the child.

These ideas gradually began to spread into the secondary system, not least in comprehensive schools which had, of course, been established to overcome the need for early classification. Many of these, as has been noted, evolved a common curriculum for the first three years of the secondary course, some introducing 'mixed ability' classes for certain activities from the start. Others had never adopted the detailed 'prismatic' streaming across the whole age-group characteristic of a few large schools. One London girls' school, Vauxhall Manor, had no system of streaming at all. Elsewhere moves in this direction now began with experiments in teaching unstreamed classes at the lower end of the school.

In 1965, the results of such an experiment undertaken in one of the large Coventry comprehensive schools were published by the headmaster who had been responsible for conducting it. On the basis of his data he concluded that both streaming and setting set arbitrary limits to the level of response of the majority of pupils. The untapped source of ability referred to in the Robbins Report would 'not be fully revealed until there is a general relaxation of streaming during the first three years in the secondary school' in favour of teaching the majority of children in a system of parallel mixed ability groups (Thompson, 1965). A large new comprehensive school which opened in Hull at this time, the David Lister school, began to operate without any streaming by ability (Rowe, 1967). Although most schools continued to use some form of ability grouping, teachers from comprehensive schools now began to exchange experiences at conferences, going on to discuss methods of teaching different subjects in a non-streamed situation (*Forum*, 1966, Vol. 9, No. 1).

Moves towards a more flexible form of organisation were reinforced by the development of new methods and, to some extent, a new approach to planning the curriculum of those aged eleven to fourteen. Team teaching, whereby up to a hundred or more pupils and several teachers worked together, was introduced in some schools, and, with this, study concentrated on a theme or series of topics which broke down the barriers between the various subjects. This implied an approach to the curriculum more integrated than is possible when each subject is taken separately for a 35 to 40 minute period. Such methods were particularly appropriate to the large comprehensive school with its variety of technical and artistic equipment. The consequent rethinking of the content of education and methods of teaching reinforced the tendency to find more flexible forms of organisation, particular for the younger age groups.

Another important factor was the introduction of the Certificate of Secondary Education (C.S.E.), especially the potentialities of 'Mode III' which permits a school to design its own curricula for examination. This pointed the way, in the view of some, to a more flexible organisation of the middle school (14-16 years), though the need to prepare for the more traditional 'O' level G.C.E. remained. Again, the 'new' sixth forms in comprehensive schools also stimulated a search for fresh patterns of organisation (*Forum*, 1967, Vol. 10, No. 1).

Despite the great expansion of higher education, there was still acute competition for university entry as the numbers in sixth forms had increased rapidly. Now the pressure of the '18 plus' on secondary schools figured as a key problem, but there was a growing awareness of these issues in the university world. The report of the Franks Committee (1966), appointed by Oxford University to consider necessary changes, recognised that hitherto entrance examinations had been geared to the organisation and practice of 'public' schools and the larger boys' grammar schools, whose educational approach and philosophy differed greatly from that of the growing number of comprehensive schools. It recommended that requirements be modified to allow recognition to the latter, as also to girls' schools and smaller grammar schools which did not stream rigidly or coach intensively for scholarships. This was to reverse the trend whereby the largest, and most selective, grammar schools had been treated as the norm to which others ought to approximate if they were to prove their capacity effectively to educate the most able children.

Account was also taken in comprehensive schools of the report of the Newsom Committee (1963)—set up some years earlier to consider the education of the 'average and below average' child, i.e. the 70 per cent or more allocated to modern schools. In fact the committee, which called its report *Half our Future*, confined its observations to some 50 per cent of children and recommended greater flexibility, special attention to the needs of the socially deprived child, and a turn outwards to the community. Although these comments bore mainly on the modern school situation they were, of course, relevant to comprehensive schools which unfortunately were not considered by the committee. Later the Plowden Report (1967) *Children and their Primary Schools* openly welcomed the demise of selection and the reduction of streaming, and advocated a gradual transition from primary to secondary school, suggesting, in particular, the establishment of 'middle schools' for children aged eight to twelve. In its evidence to this committee the National Union of Teachers expressed full support for comprehensive reorganisation, now a matter of union policy. Associations of secondary teachers remained, on the whole, opposed. But in 1967 the Assistant Masters' Association published a revision of an earlier report by members engaged in teaching in comprehensive schools. It included positive assessments on some of the most disputed points. For instance :

The benefits of being in a sixth form are, in a comprehensive school, open to a wider range of pupils than in any grammar school. A consensus of opinions ex-

pressed at one of our conferences was: 'All the traditional methods used to develop personal qualities,
encourage judgment, etc. could be applied successfully
to many more pupils than previously. It was felt that
the comprehensive school would probably do this better
than the average grammar school because of its size
and the consequent wider variety of opportunities' . . .
A comprehensive school's sixth form is an open society
(A.M.A., 1967, 98).

Past, present and future

At this stage, it may be suggested, comprehensive schools
were beginning to come into their own as educational
institutions. These were not schools provided for the people
'from above, in a form and with a content of studies that
suited the ruling interests'; rather they offered signs of
'the growth of a genuine popular philosophy of education',
a belief that the basic schools of the nation should realise
new and 'clearly conceived social and cultural purposes',
as Sir Fred Clarke had argued was so necessary a quarter
of a century before.

This is not to say that there was an end to controversy,
or to differences about the procedure of comprehensive
reorganisation. In drawing up plans local authorities had
many vital decisions to take, some of which had barely
been discussed on other than administrative grounds. For
instance, does comprehensive education necessarily imply
co-education? Some have thought so, others not; a halfway
house is to provide alternatives (as at Coventry) whereas
hitherto in some areas single sex schools have been the
rule.

A few authorities, anxious to move rapidly, sometimes
after earlier frustrations, advanced plans which were
characterised as makeshift and as open to criticism on
various counts; some of these were returned by the Depart-

ment of Education for revision. A few authorities, on the other hand, for instance Doncaster and Cardiff, proposed to continue parallel secondary schools with different leaving ages, involving selection by 'guided parental choice' at thirteen or fourteen; this, it has been suggested, may result in a dangerous form of social selection and has come to be regarded as acceptable only as a transitional measure. The sixth form colleges, of which quite a number are planned, take different forms. Some authorities are developing colleges for full-time students only, mostly preparing for 'A' level examinations, others have planned for the 'junior college', covering all full-time and part-time provision for the sixteen to eighteen age groups.

A matter of particular concern to the larger urban authorities is that differences may develop between comprehensive schools in socially favoured and socially deprived areas, and whether such differences can be obviated by defining the catchment area for each school so that it draws on a representative social range. This became a focal point of criticism once reorganisation had been announced as general policy, critics suggesting that the 'neighbourhood' school in downtown areas would be socially segregated by comparison with grammar schools which drew on all sections of the community. This standpoint, however, failed to take into account the fact that many modern schools were in fact already situated in socially deprived areas, as the Newsom Committee had stressed.

In reply it has been argued that the comprehensive school should, in general, be a neighbourhood school and that this can be one of its main strengths. At Bristol, for instance, schools on new housing estates have developed as community schools with the support of the local authority. Not only do they provide for all the children living nearby, but they also foster and provide accommodation for youth groups, adult classes, the community council and cultural activities of various kinds; libraries have been enlarged and opened to the public at week-ends and during school holidays (*Trends in Education*, April 1967). This is to realise in a new context one of the most fruitful community developments of the 1930s, the Cambridgeshire village colleges inspired by Henry Morris.

The decision to unify the publicly provided system of secondary education also threw into new relief the position of the independent schools, and, in 1966, a commission was appointed to consider and report on the subject. Behind the maintained grammar schools there have stood a special class of school maintained by 'direct grant' from the Department of Education (and so not under the aegis of local authorities). Some direct grant schools are highly selective and have greatly influenced local systems of education down to the primary level (Allsop and Grugeon, 1966). Behind these stood the independent schools including the leading 'public' schools. The point to be made here is that in 1902 it was these schools which were the most influential, the national system of secondary schools being designed in their image. By the 1960s that position had been reversed as the principle of segregation came into question. Sociological studies of these schools and their ethos began to accumulate. One, *Winchester and the Public School Élite* (1967), found that the 'career advantages of individuals with élite family backgrounds have not diminished since the late nineteenth century', confirming earlier findings about continuance of 'the prevailing and long-standing high self-recruitment of the upper class' (Bishop and Williamson, 216). This indicates that there have been social reasons for retaining segregation as strong as those for eliminating it.

To follow the progress of the comprehensive school from idea to reality is, then, to raise most of the major questions about the educational system. These have only been touched upon in this survey, the main aim of which has been to trace the development of the comprehensive school itself. It seems likely that the provision of a fully comprehensive system of secondary education will take many years to complete in all its details. But in the history of English education, the buildings, the administrative problems, have never been the decisive factors. In the years after 1870 the schools, designed to provide 'sound and cheap' elementary instruction for the working class grew 'higher tops'. School Boards required to provide merely elementary teaching built and fostered Higher Grade Schools. After the 1902 Act had cut back this development and left the schools for the majority enclosed within the elementary system, there developed central and junior technical schools and the beginnings of senior departments, so that in 1926 the Hadow Committee could recommend that senior schools be universally established. After 1944 the secondary modern schools, cut off from access to external examinations and allocated only those pupils not considered capable of following a full secondary course, broke through the administrative and psychological barriers. So also comprehensive schools transcended the divisions of the selective system and pointed the way to a general transformation, despite many material difficulties at first such as accommodation in separate buildings designed for other purposes.

Within the framework of advances during recent years —the new developments in junior schools, the great expansion of sixth forms, the growing flexibility of the examination system, the expansion of higher education— the comprehensive school has the opportunity to realise a new concept of the nature and function of secondary education. It has already begun to do so by recasting curricula, introducing a greater measure of pupil participation at various levels, and forging new links between pupils and teachers, between school and neighbourhood. A beginning has also been made in modifying streaming as new ways of fostering learning are sought, with the aid of resources which can help to revolutionise school life. It may well be that the educational discussions and experiments now under way will bring greater, or more significant, changes than those which have brought into being the comprehensive school.

7
Postscript, 1966–1972

Quite early in the Labour government's term of office the government declared its intention to bring to an end divisions along tripartite lines in secondary education and to introduce comprehensive schooling. This was made clear both in a House of Commons resolution in January 1965, and in Circular 10/65. In spite of a full five-year term of office, however, this intention was only very partially achieved by June 1970, when the Labour government was defeated at the general election. In the meantime the Conservative party had hardened its line on this reform. Although its official spokesman on education—Edward Boyle—had clearly stated that, if the Conservatives were restored to office, Circular 10/65 would remain in being, in 1969 Edward Heath announced that 10/65 would be withdrawn at the earliest opportunity. This policy formed part of the Tory election programme, and the first act of the new Conservative government was to issue Circular 10/70— less than one month after the election. Circular 10/70 in effect withdrew 10/65, in that it removed any pressure from the central government to 'go comprehensive'.

These events are a reminder that educational issues, particularly where they concern the fate of existing institutions, can seldom be removed from politics—that they are, in some respects, directly political questions. Decisions about schools and schooling are not always determined on educational criteria alone. As comprehensive schools multiplied in the mid-late 1960s, so opposition (particularly from supporters of grammar schools) hardened, to reach a climax with the publication of the sensational Black Papers on education, directed to Members of Parliament. These three publications, which appeared in 1969-70, linked comprehensive education with student unrest and the primary school 'revolution' as all leading to anarchy and a decline in 'standards'. Precisely what effect this movement, and the new government's policy had on the development of comprehensive education is hard to say.

The Labour government, 1964-70

Circular 10/65, it is first worth noting, had no statutory power. It did not and could not imply any legal sanction to establish comprehensive schools. Anthony Crosland, then Secretary of State for Education and Science, has since revealed that its actual formulation—in terms of 'requesting' rather than 'requiring' local authorities to submit plans within a year—was the result of his own personal decision arrived at after discussion (Kogan, 1971, 189). A request can, of course, be turned down, and a few local authorities maintained this latter position throughout the period; no statutory sanction could be used against them. Pressure was further applied through the issue a year later (in March 1966) of a further Circular—Circular 10/66, which laid down that resources would not be forthcoming for any building in secondary education which did not contribute to (or form part of) a scheme of comprehensive reorganisation; in this way the D.E.S. was able to use its financial powers to 'persuade' local authorities to go comprehensive. This pressure (which was perfectly legitimate, and had been used also in the 1920s to persuade recalcitrant local authorities to complete Hadow reorganisation) had some effect in that a few of these authorities now agreed to produce comprehensive schemes. But overall the position dragged on, authorities which wished to delay even planning a transition (which was all they were asked to do) were able to do so with impunity. Indeed, towards the close of its period of office—in the spring of 1970—the Labour government did introduce a bill which, had it passed through Parliament, would have added teeth to its intentions—in the form of a legal sanction. However, due to mismanagement, the Bill failed, to be followed by the government's electoral defeat in the summer.

What, then, was achieved during the five years 1965 to 1970? The total number of comprehensive schools, which had doubled between 1960 and 1965 (from 130 to 262), increased between four to five times to 1,145. The percentage of the secondary school population in comprehensive schools grew from 8.5 per cent in 1965 to 31 per cent in 1970—an increase of just less than four times. (See Table 1.) Just under a third of secondary school pupils were, by 1970, in comprehensive schools. If the reform was far from fully achieved, a substantial breakthrough had been made. This is the more evident when projections for the future are taken into account, since local authorities who wished to introduce comprehensive systems were not always able to do so immediately for local reasons concerning the availability of schools and school buildings. In 1972 it was estimated that, provided local authorities' plans then in being were implemented, 1,825 comprehensive schools would be in existence in 1973, attended by approximately 48 per cent of the secondary school population.

But these figures do not present the whole story by any means. Surveys in the late 1960s showed that only a proportion of these schools were 'genuine' comprehensive

108.

TABLE 1 Growth of comprehensive schools in England and Wales, 1950-73

Year	1950	1955	1960	1965	1966	1967	1968	1969	1970	1971	1972	1973*
Number of schools	10	16	130	262	387	507	748	960	1145	1373	1591	1825*
Percentage of secondary-school population in comprehensive schools	0·3	0·6	4·7	8·5	11·1	14·4	20·9	26	31	38	44*	48*

* Figures and percentages for these years approximate only. For 1960 to 1968 percentages given by Minister of State for Education and Science, House of Commons, 15 May 1969. Percentages for 1950 and 1955, and numbers of schools from 1950 to 1970, derived from, or given in, D.E.S., Statistics, vol. I, p. viii, 1968 and vol. I, 1970. (From C. Benn and B. Simon, Half Way There, 2nd ed. 1972, p. 102, reproduced by kind permission of McGraw Hill Book Company and of Penguin Books. Figures for 1971-3 modified in the light of later information.)

schools—in the sense that they took in *all* the children from the locality, and were not 'creamed by' or 'coexisting with' selective grammar schools. In terms of the total number of pupils attending secondary schools, only some 12 per cent attended 'genuinely' comprehensive schools—not the full 31 per cent given earlier who attended 'comprehensive' schools in 1970. In London, for instance, where there are over 80 comprehensive schools, some 40 'voluntary aided' or 'assisted' grammar schools also exist all of which take in pupils financed by the local authority—these schools (for the most part denominational) take a selective entry, providing for 17 per cent of London's secondary school pupils, so that the comprehensive schools do not receive anything near a comprehensive intake. The same is true of the 16 comprehensive schools at Coventry, of the 23 comprehensive schools in Bristol, and elsewhere. In fact 'coexistence' has come to be seen as one of the major problems arising from comprehensive reorganisation. Many of these grammar schools are not directly under the control of the local authorities concerned, and it would require legislation to bring them into comprehensive systems. This applies not only to the so-called 'voluntary aided' grammar schools in London and elsewhere, but also, and particularly, to the 179 direct grant grammar schools which are financed directly by the D.E.S.

Figure 1 indicates clearly that the growth of the comprehensive sector took place during this period largely at the expense of the secondary modern schools, and that the grammar schools, up to 1970, have not been centrally involved in reorganisation schemes. Between 1961 and 1970, the proportion of secondary school pupils attending comprehensive schools (as indicated in this Table) has increased from 4 per cent to 29 per cent of the school population—by about 25 per cent. But the bulk of these pupils come from secondary modern schools whose share

Figure 1   Secondary Education 1961–1970
Percentage of total pupil population in secondary education,
England and Wales*

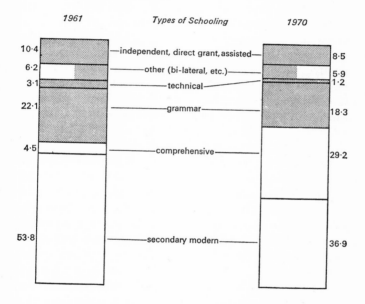

Shaded areas: selective, fee paying or independent sector
Clear areas: non-selective sector

1961   Types of Schooling   1970

10·4 —independent, direct grant, assisted— 8·5
6·2 — other (bi-lateral, etc.) — 5·9
3·1 —technical— 1·2
22·1 —grammar— 18·3
4·5 —comprehensive— 29·2
53·8 —secondary modern— 36·9

* 1961 figures from p. 124, *Social Trends*, H.M.S.O., 1970; 1970 figures from vol. 1, p. 2, D.E.S. *Statistics*, 1970. (From *Half Way There*, 2nd ed. 1972, p. 86, reproduced by kind permission of McGraw Hill Book Company and of Penguin Books.) The discrepancy of 2 per cent—compared with Table 1—in the proportion of secondary school pupils attending comprehensive schools in 1970 arises from differences in the definition of secondary school population in the source data.

of the secondary school population over this period has declined by some 17 per cent. The share of the grammar schools, on the other hand, has declined only by something under 3 per cent—while separate technical schools have been virtually obliterated. There is also a 2 per cent decline in the share of independent, direct grant and assisted schools, making a total of about 5 per cent for the grammar school sector. Despite the growth of comprehensive schools, therefore, the grammar schools have not, as yet, experienced any radical change.

There are several reasons for the Labour government's relative failure to carry out its declared intention. The initial decision neither to legislate—which would have provided a firm statutory basis for change—nor to formulate the Circular in much stronger terms meant that initially reliance was placed on comprehensive education as a policy commanding a general consensus. However it may have seemed in 1965, this did not work out in practice, but by the time this was realised it was too late to take drastic action—or so it may be argued. An additional factor lay in the normal swing in municipal elections during the period of the Labour government, though in this case the swing was more marked than usual. By 1969 Labour had lost control of almost every important city and county borough in the country, the great majority of which, in 1964-5, were firmly under its control. While Conservative authorities did not normally revert to a tripartite system involving selection once a comprehensive system had been established (Manchester is a case in point)—where Labour authorities, hoping for a local consensus, were slow off the mark, reorganisation was delayed and then denied. Indeed, as the difficulties with which the Labour government was faced on a national and international scale mounted during the late 1960s, it became increasingly evident that they were not prepared for a confrontation with local authorities, now largely under Tory rule, on this issue—though the Bill introduced in 1970 did mark a final (if half-hearted) attempt to speed things up.

The same was true of the government's approach to the question of coexistence, and in particular to the direct grant schools. No plans were made for legislation to make possible the integration of voluntary-aided grammar schools in comprehensive systems, reliance being once again placed on consensus agreement—a policy which had signally failed in London over the whole post-war period. The problems posed by the existence of the direct grant schools —a powerful grouping of prestigious and religious founda-tions—were finally relegated to a Commission of enquiry, which reported early in 1970—the Donnison Commis-sion. Although this report strongly favoured bringing these schools into local systems of comprehensive education, no steps were taken to implement the proposals. On this count also, the Labour government's record is one of failure in relation to declared intentions.

Nevertheless, as we have seen, there was something of a breakthrough, at least in certain areas of the country, where determined local authorities were able to make headway. In 1969, for instance, Leicestershire, not a Labour controlled county council, completed its pioneering two-tier system of comprehensive education, being the first English county finally to abolish the 11-plus throughout its area. All schools in the county now formed part of the comprehensive system (with the exception of the direct grant schools at Loughborough). Manchester and Sheffield were two of several large urban authorities which did likewise, and, by 1972, a total of 46 (out of 163) local authorities in England and Wales could boast complete (or almost complete) comprehensive systems. Success on this level in some parts of the country—both urban and rural—offset to some extent the overall failure of the original plans. Certainly by the end of the period, a quite substantial proportion both of children and schools were comprehensive'—and aspiring towards the status of genuinely comprehensive schools. By this time also, most authorities at least had plans for making the transition to comprehensive education.

The system now coming into being bore little resemblance, in some important respects, to early ideas as to comprehensive reorganisation—and even to the proposals in Circular 10/65 itself. That Circular, while presenting various options (see p. 95), specifically recommended 'all-through', 11-18 schools as the most desirable type to be established, whether through new building, or by the merging of existing buildings. Both types 3 and 4 (p. 95)—the sixth form college (16-18) and the middle school followed by an upper school (9-13, 13-18)—were regarded as strictly experimental, and warning was given that only 'a very small number' of such schemes would be approved.

But, in fact, over the five-year period opinion among local authorities and the D.E.S. changed quite radically as to the two latter schemes, and, as we shall see, many such schemes are already in being and others are planned. Table 2 although drawn up in 1968 (and based on data then available) shows that, of the 3,995 schools actually planned by local authorities, 38 per cent were to be 11-18 schools, 25 per cent involved middle schools of one kind or another (though this category does not include 8-12 middle schools already in being in some areas), and as many as 32 per cent involved separate provision for the sixth form, whether in the form of a sixth form college (9 per cent) or of transfer to a school acting as a sixth form centre to coexisting 11-16 schools. These, then, are the three main types of systems coming into being, and, although in 1972, 56 per cent of all comprehensive schools were of the 11-18 variety (*Half*

114

TABLE 2 *Future reorganisation pattern—England and Wales*
Based on local authority long-term plans operating, approved and submitted by 1968*

Type of scheme		Number of existing schools involved in planned schemes, 1968		Percentage of total planned schools
All-through	11/12–18	1524		38% All-through
Tiered	9–13/13–18	792	20%	25% Tiered
	11–14/14–18	197	5%	
Separate Sixth	11/12–16+Sixth form college	374	9%	32% Separate Sixth
	11/12–16 coexisting with 11/12–18	901	23%	
Selective Interim	11/12–15/16 coexisting 13/14–18	207		5% Selective Interim
Total		3995		100%

*For further information, see The Comprehensive Schools Committee's *Comprehensive Reorganization Survey, 1968/9*, p. 6, from which this table is derived. (From *Half Way There*, 2nd ed. 1972, p. 115, reproduced by kind permission of McGraw Hill Book Company and of Penguin Books.)

Way There, p. 125), this percentage is likely to fall along the lines indicated in the projections above.

So far from introducing a monolithic system of education throughout the country, as was once alleged to be the inevitable result of comprehensive education, a main characteristic of the present phase is the *variety* of systems now being established. With the development of 8-12 schools (as recommended by the Plowden Council), of 9-13 schools (as pioneered at Bradford and by the West Riding), of 10-14 schools (as developed recently in Leicestershire), of 11-14 and 11-16 schools in some areas, of 12-16 schools (a popular variant when combined with sixth form colleges), of 12-18 schools alongside 11-18 schools, and of 16-18 schools (or sixth form colleges proper), the educational system of the country is being converted into a mosaic·of different patterns.

The actual educational effects of this variety, and the relative merits of each system, are matters well worthy of discussion—though this is not a question that we can enter here. One important issue raised, however, is the clear importance of establishing criteria for staffing and equipment in relation to each age level; without this there is a danger of a deterioration in standards in respect of these essential conditions. In terms of the objectives of comprehensive education, it may, perhaps, be said that all such systems can meet the essential criterion of comprehensive education—free and open access to each succeeding stage for all pupils, without any form of academic or social selection. Where open entry is allowed in relation to sixth form colleges (as at Southampton and elsewhere), these clearly form parts of comprehensive systems of schooling; where academic tests restrict entry, however, as is the case in relation to certain sixth form colleges, these cannot be regarded as truly comprehensive systems.

Return of the Tories, 1970-2

With the reform less than halfway completed, in 1970, a Conservative government was elected pledged to withdraw Circular 10/65. As we have already seen, this was the first act of the new government, although the 'withdrawal' took the form of the publication of another circular (10/70) which announced no specific policy. Instead it stated that local authorities would 'now be freer to determine the shape of secondary provision in their areas', and that proposals would be judged on 'educational considerations in general, local needs and wishes in particular, and the wise use of resources'. Immediate reaction among teachers' organisations and in the educational press and elsewhere was hostile to this development, which was seen as an attack on comprehensive education and in particular, an invitation to local authorities to 'reconsider' comprehensive plans. Many resolutions of protest were passed by teachers' organisations and others at this stage, some now supporting comprehensive education definitely for the first time. This immediate and sharp reaction was a clear indication that the introduction of comprehensive education had rallied wide support both among educationists and the general public.

The immediate result, paradoxically, was a strengthening of the movement for comprehensive education, especially in areas which were on the verge of deciding on this transition, but had not already made it. Some of these were areas under Conservative control—as, for instance, Bedfordshire. The procedure now used by the Secretary of State in considering schemes submitted for approval was that under Section 13 of the 1944 Education Act—which involves looking at the position of *every* school in a reorganisation plan individually. In October 1972, Mrs Thatcher announced that she had refused to allow authorities to carry out their proposals (in spite of the terms of Circular 10/70) in as many as ninety-two cases—these, she claimed, were largely cases of 'famous or well known grammar schools' which the local authorities wished to merge into comprehensive systems, but on which she had received protests from local people. At the same time she was reported as 'pleading for those who believed intensely in the future of grammar schools to be vocal in their areas' (*Times Educational Supplement*, 20 October 1972). In general it was hard to find any clear policy behind the Secretary of State's decisions in relation to specific schools up to this time—some schemes were allowed, others disallowed, perhaps according to the degree of local objections received by the Minister. But to uphold objections in relation even to one grammar school in a local scheme for comprehensive education can effectively prevent the scheme as a whole from coming into being.

On the other hand, a few days after Mrs Thatcher's statement, a government spokesman (Lord Belstead) claimed that comprehensive reorganisation was in fact going ahead at a good speed. Lord Belstead's intervention was made specifically to counter a survey by the National Foundation for Educational Research, published in October 1972, which claimed that the move to comprehensive education was slowing down. The N.F.E.R. found that 64 per cent of 11-year-old children were still undergoing some form of selection for secondary education—about the proportion that would be expected in the light of the data given earlier; they found also, however, that, of 104 local authorities forecasted in 1968 to be likely to abolish selection procedures by 1972, only 24 had in fact done so. Further, they add, 'the picture for the next few years is one of only very gradual movement towards comprehensive education, many authorities continuing to maintain mixed systems of selective and comprehensive schools' (*Educa-*

tional Research News, September 1972). In general the N.F.E.R. found 50 authorities not operating any form of selection procedure; 56 operating selection procedures in part of their areas; and 55 which still operated selection procedures over the whole of their area. This information tallies with the most recent authoritative survey of the overall position, which estimates that, overall, there were in 1972 a total of 1,591 comprehensive schools in Britain, catering for 44 per cent of the secondary school population aged 11 and over (Table 1).

The transition to comprehensive education is certainly still taking place, in spite of the fact that it is no longer government policy. Important local authorities such as Birmingham, Leicester and Liverpool now have comprehensive plans; and this is true of many authorities which delayed the transition in the 1960s whatever their political complexion. Indeed the movement towards comprehensive education is bigger than particular political parties, and, as we have seen in earlier chapters, has taken shape historically without the support of any of the major parties. Fundamentally this movement is a reflection of deep-seated economic and social changes. It seems unlikely that it can now be reversed, but, as throughout its chequered history, its path is far from easy, and many obstacles still remain to be surmounted before a system of genuinely comprehensive schools covers the country.

Inside the schools, 1966-72

As more and more comprehensive schools are being brought into being, significant developments have been taking place within the schools themselves, to which some attention should be devoted. First, and perhaps most important, has been the move towards flexible forms of grouping, and particularly the decline of rigid streaming procedures

TABLE 3 First-year grouping by type of school in Britain, 1968, and 1971 sample survey (schools with 11- and 12-plus intake only)

Method of grouping	Percentage of schools (numbers in brackets)					Total number of schools	Percentage 1968	1971 Sample survey Percentage of schools
	11/12-18 (I)	11/12-18 (II)	11/12-16	11/12-13	11/12-14/15			
1 In streams	17·5	13	20·5	34	23	130	19·5	4·5
2 In broad ability bands	34·5	32	27	21	26	210	31	45
3 In sets	4		8	7	10	36	5·5	3·5
4 Combination of streams and sets	12	16	18	14	17	96	14·5	5·5
5 Mixed ability (1) (no more than two subjects settled)	5	10	8	14	1	42	6	10
6 Mixed ability (2) (remedial pupils separated)	14	13	9·5	10	7	80	12	18
7 Mixed ability (3) (for all subjects and pupils)	5	6	2		6	29	4	6·5
8 Other method	7	10	6	6	6	43	6·5	7
Unknown	1		1		4	7	1	
Total number of schools	100 (389)	100 (31)	100 (154)	100 (29)	100 (70)	673	100·0	100·0 (111)

(From *Half Way There*, 2nd ed. 1972, p. 219, reproduced by kind permission of McGraw Hill Book Company and of Penguin Books.)

(typical of the early schools) in favour of systems of broad banding and of various types of mixed ability grouping. Table 3 (from *Half Way There*, p. 219), is based on a survey of 76 per cent of all schools existing in 1968 and of a representative sample of the same schools late in 1971. Although this indicates that, in 1968, about 40 per cent of schools used streaming, setting, or a combination of both (categories 1, 3, 4) as the form of grouping during the first year, by 1971 this percentage had dropped to only 13·5 per cent, a reduction to one third in three years. On the other hand, schools using one of the three forms of mixed ability grouping (categories 5, 6, 7) rose over the same period from 22 per cent to 34·5 per cent. This is a remarkable development considering that mixed ability grouping was regarded as impracticable by most teachers and educationists some ten years ago. Banding, however—a method by which pupils are grouped into 3 or perhaps 4 broad bands—remains the most popular form of organisation, the percentage of schools using this system rising from 31 per cent to 45 per cent between 1968 and 1971. It seems likely that the dramatic decline in rigid streaming systems (from 19·5 per cent to 4·5 per cent) as well as of setting has resulted in a transition to broad banding in many schools, while a significant number have moved to one or other of the three systems of mixed ability grouping. Of these, the most radical (in terms of innovation) is that defined under category 7, where all pupils, including slow learners or 'remedial' pupils, are taught together in mixed ability groups for all subjects. In the latter case slow learners may be withdrawn for specific tuition by the remedial staff in the basic skills, though remaining part of a mixed ability group, or, as several schools are now attempting, the remedial staff works with slow learning pupils in the normal class or group learning situation.

While a significant number of schools are now organised

on the basis of mixed ability grouping in the first year, a survey in 1968 showed that a proportion of these maintain this system into the second year, and a smaller percentage into the third year. Indeed several schools are now attempting to maintain this system of grouping right through the school, including the fourth and fifth years. C.S.E. Mode III examinations, and the development of Mode III G.C.E. now make this a practical possibility, and recent evidence indicates that, where this is done, examination results may actually be improved (*Half Way There*, pp. 228-9). It may be said that, where schools are able successfully to develop procedures which reduce the segregation of pupils to a minimum, as these schools are doing, the full advantages of comprehensive reorganisation are being achieved.

This development is closely linked to plans for raising the school leaving age, and with the proposal of the Schools Council for the substitution of a single examination at 16 for the present two (G.C.E. and C.S.E.). If the latter scheme is brought into being it will make easier the unification of the middle years of the comprehensive schools, although, since the new examination is being planned only for 60 per cent of the age group, some teachers fear that it may well introduce a new divisive factor into the internal organisation of comprehensive schools. Many comprehensive school heads hold that it should be possible now to devise an examination appropriate to all pupils at this age, and were this done, it should make it possible to avoid divisions within the schools. The raising of the age to 16, however, now makes it possible for comprehensive schools to plan a full five-year course for the majority of their pupils—though about a third, unfortunately, will still leave school before completing the full five years.

The raising of the school age and the provision of a single examination at 16 both help towards the provision of a common curriculum—or better, common educational experiences—for all children, a matter referred to earlier (p. 77). The content of the curriculum is now under much discussion, and comprehensive schools are participating actively in the many curriculum reform schemes launched by the Schools Council and Nuffield. The tendency is towards the development of interdisciplinary curricula, together with the use of the resources approach to learning, involving the substitution of much group and individual work for the more traditional forms of class teaching. For these new forms of organising and stimulating learning mixed ability grouping often provides the most appropriate method; and partly for this reason the tendency is towards the reduction of streaming and class teaching. This movement in itself promotes new relations between teachers and pupils, particularly in so far as the teacher's role is changing from that of ultimate authority to that of motivating, facilitating and structuring the pupil's own discovery and search for knowledge. The tendency, then, in common with other contemporary social trends, is towards the more 'open' school, as defined effectively by Basil Bernstein in a well-known article in *New Society* (14 September 1967).

Together with these new forms of organising learning, by which teachers tend to work together more as teams than individually, has gone a move towards teacher and pupil participation in government and control. This takes the form of the establishment of school councils, involving representation from both pupils and staff, and of the devolvement of greater responsibility to members of staff than has been the case in the past. This latter movement has been taken furthest at Countesthorpe College in Leicestershire, an upper school (and community college) where all decisions as to the running of the school have been delegated by the head to the staff as a whole, although, under the present articles of government, the head retains final responsibility for the school's functioning. It is no accident that this school is also based on the resources approach to learning and mixed ability grouping throughout.

These are not, of course, the only new developments now taking place. Sixth form colleges, or secondary colleges, as some are called, are now coming into being in various parts of the country and it will not be long before significant new developments are likely to be reported from these new-type institutions. In some areas also (for instance Exeter and Barnstaple) the 16-19 age group now attends at the local technical college where all full-time and part-time work over 16 is concentrated. It is too early yet to attempt any evaluation of this move, but it is certain to be watched with interest.

At the other end of the age range new middle schools of various types—8-12, 9-13, and 10-14—have been established in the last few years, and, as we have seen, these schools are likely to form part of the school experience of up to a third of the age group in the near future. Much discussion has taken place before these schools have been set up, and many important educational issues hammered out by teacher groups in the areas where they have been established—for instance in Southampton, the West Riding and elsewhere. The main interest here lies in the methods being developed in these schools to fuse together the different primary and secondary school traditions—the former based on class teaching for all activities, the latter on the specialist work of the traditional secondary school. With the tendency for secondary education to move towards interdisciplinary, and sometimes towards integrated, studies, together with the relaxation of streaming, both traditions are, in fact, tending to merge. The establishment of middle schools on a large scale may well accelerate this process, and so lead towards the unification of education as an

124

organic whole. However since little information about these schools is yet available, it is too early as yet to make any firm predictions as to the future.

Conclusion

Projections as to the future, based on local authority plans, indicate that the impetus towards comprehensive reorganisation, generated in the 1960s, will continue into the mid-1970s, but, perhaps, with waning intensity. In 1971 about 1,000 comprehensive schools were planned to open between 1972 and 1975, but some 600 of these had no firm date for opening. A chief reason for this delay is lack of finance for building, and, at the time of writing (December 1972) the government's plans indicate that the freeze on secondary school building imposed two years ago will continue right up to 1980— the total sum allocated for new secondary school building over this entire period, according to the White Paper issued at this time, amounting to no more than £20,000,000, or sufficient only for one new secondary school in each authority's area as an absolute maximum (*Education: A Framework for Expansion*, Cmnd 5174). If this policy is adhered to throughout the 1970s, it will act as a major factor preventing advance towards comprehensive education in many areas. However, forward planning of this type can never be certain, since economic or political changes may open up new perspectives.

That the trend towards comprehensive education will continue is certain; the doubt is as to how far it will go, and how complete reorganisation will prove. The present government is clearly concerned to give increased financial aid to the direct grant schools, while the independent sector, remains outside any local authority's plans. If this trend continues it may be that in the long run local authority systems will be largely comprehensive, while the independent and direct grant sector remains untouched and highly selective.

But even here it is impossible to make predictions. The impetus towards reorganisation has recently gathered pace and may do so again, in spite of a certain disenchantment engendered by such studies as Julienne Ford's *Social Class and the Comprehensive School* (1970) which seemed to indicate that such schools were not overcoming social inequalities. The answer to this criticism by comprehensive school proponents was twofold: first, that comprehensive schools were not established to bring about an egalitarian society, but to provide increased educational opportunities for the mass of the children, previously excluded from systematic forms of secondary education by the 11-plus examination. Second, that in order to achieve this, selection through streaming within individual schools must be modified in parallel with the abolition of separate schools for separate groups of children.

That there is a move in this direction has been shown in this chapter; but even so, the more flexible methods resulting from the abandonment of streaming (in particular the use of group and individual work) can work both ways; such methods can either reduce differentiation or they can be used to increase divisions between pupils without on the surface appearing to do so. Such developments must therefore be kept under review, both as concerns their long-term effects and short-term consequences.

Whereas in the past the successful establishment of a system of comprehensive schools was seen as the end to be aimed at, today there is at least equal concern that these schools, once established, should not perpetuate selection and differentiation under new names, but consciously set out to ensure that all pupils are given equal opportunity to master knowledge and skills and to develop their talents and interests. To achieve this requires fundamental changes in the organisation of teaching and learning. Given the opportunity, in terms of material conditions, teaching power and finance, it seems that the schools are now sufficiently well based and confident to make further advances towards this objective.

8 Suggestions for further reading

An excellent account of the history of secondary education from 1902 and of the early movement for the comprehensive school is Olive Banks' *Parity and Prestige in English Education* (Routledge and Kegan Paul, 1955). This may be supplemented by the books by E. J. R. Eaglesham and G. Bernbaum mentioned in the Preface (p. xii). Robin Pedley's *The Comprehensive School* (Penguin Books, 1963, new ed. 1966) contains historical material and much else of interest.

Comprehensive Planning (Councils and Education Press, 1965), edited by Stuart Maclure, gives plans for secondary school re-organisation, with some historical background, in eleven local authority areas, while S. C. Mason *The Leicestershire Experiment* (Councils and Education Press), first published in 1957 and revised several times, is indispensable for an understanding of the two-tier system.

The N.U.T. symposium, *Inside the Comprehensive School* (1958), contains chapters dealing with all aspects of the schools by head-teachers; in *Comprehensive Schools in Action* (Oldbourne, 1964), Roger Cole gives a useful account of the functioning of a particular school. Other accounts of London schools by headmistresses are H. Chetwynd, *Comprehensive School* (Routledge, 1960) and Margaret Miles, *Comprehensive Schooling, problems and perspectives* (Longmans, 1968). G. C. Firth's *Comprehensive Schools in Coventry and Elsewhere* (Coventry Education Committee, 1963) analyses the evolution of the Coventry schools as well as their internal academic and social organisation. The Inner London Education Authority's *London Comprehensive Schools 1966* (1967) may usefully be compared with the L.C.C.'s survey of 1961 (see bibliography).

On grammar schools, in addition to books mentioned in the text, see F. Stevens, *The Living Tradition* (Hutchinson, 1960) and B.

Jackson and D. Marsden, *Education and the Working Class* (Routledge and Kegan Paul, 1962). *The Secondary Modern School* (Faber, 1963), by William Taylor, should be supplemented by *Secondary Modern*, by H. Loukes (Harrap, 1956) and H. C. Dent's *Secondary Modern Schools* (Routledge and Kegan Paul, 1958). Journals which have carried material particularly on comprehensive education include *Forum*, *Where* (published by the Advisory Centre for Education), and *Comprehensive Education*, the journal of the Comprehensive Schools Committee. But there is much to be found in other educational journals listed in the bibliography while many of the books also listed are indispensable for a full study of the subject.

Postscript (1972)

Since the first edition of this book was prepared (1968) there have been many publications on comprehensive schools. The most important of these are included in the bibliography, but reference may be made here to the three reports published by the National Foundation for Educational Research, each arising from the research commissioned by the D.E.S. in 1966. These are *Comprehensive Education in England and Wales*, ed. T. G. Monks (1968) which surveyed 331 schools in existence in 1966, *Comprehensive Education in Action*, ed. T. G. Monks (1970) which concentrated on certain aspects of 59 of these schools, and a final 'evaluative' report based on a study of only 12 schools, *A Critical Appraisal of Comprehensive Education* (1972). Also based on survey material, but from a total of 728 comprehensive schools in existence by 1968 is *Half-Way There* (1970), by Caroline Benn and Brian Simon; a second edition of this book with new material based on additional surveys was published by Penguin in 1972. These two sources, together with the annual surveys of comprehensive reorganisation plans by Caroline Benn for the Comprehensive Schools Committee (later renamed the Campaign for Comprehensive Education) make available a great deal of material on almost every aspect of comprehensive education.

A number of books dealing with individual schools have also been published, of which S. King's *Ten Years All In* (1969) and Albert Rowe's *The School as a Guidance Community* (1971) are examples. Useful case studies of the transition to comprehensive education include *Going Comprehensive*, by Richard Batley *et al.* (1970) and *Becoming Comprehensive*, edited by Elizabeth Halsall (1970). A critical assessment of the Labour government's achievement is made by Dennis Marsden in a Fabian Tract entitled *Politicians, Comprehensives and Equality* (1971). The three Black

SUGGESTIONS FOR FURTHER READING

Papers referred to in the final chapter were published in 1969 and 1970 and are entitled *The Fight for Education* (1969), *The Crisis in Education* (1969) and *Goodbye Mr. Short* (1970), all edited by C. B. Cox and A. E. Dyson. *Education for Democracy*, edited by David Rubinstein and Colin Stoneman was published as a Penguin Education Special (1970) as a specific reply to the Black Papers, a second (revised) edition being published in 1972. Other recent books are listed in the bibliography, but special attention should be drawn to Elizabeth Halsall's *The Comprehensive School: guidelines for the reorganisation of secondary education* (1973), and the second report of the Public Schools Commission (Donnison Commission, 1970).

Bibliography

Official reports and documents

Board of Education (1899-1944)
    (1928) *The New Prospect in Education*
    (1937) *Handbook of Suggestions for Teachers*
    (1939) *Education in 1938 (annual report)*
    (1941) *Education after the War* ('Green Book')
    (1943) *Educational Reconstruction* (*White Paper*)

Consultative Committee to the Board of Education (1899-1944)
    (1924) *Tests of Educable Capacity*
    (1926) *The Education of the Adolescent* (Hadow Report)
    (1931) *The Primary School* (Hadow)
    (1938) *Secondary Education, with special reference to Grammar Schools and Technical High Schools* (Spens Report)

Secondary School Examinations Council (Established 1917)
    (1943) *Curriculum and Examinations in Secondary Schools* (Norwood Report)

Ministry of Education (1944-1964)
    (1945) *The Nation's Schools, their plan and purpose. Pamphlet No. 1*
    (1945) *A Guide to the Educational System of England and Wales. Pamphlet No. 2*
    (1945) 'The Organisation of Secondary Schools', Circular 73. December
    (1946) 'Examinations in Secondary Schools', Circular 103. May
    (1947) 'The Organisation of Secondary Education'. Circular 144. June
    (1947) *The New Secondary Education. Pamphlet No. 9*
    (1951) *The Road to the Sixth Form. Pamphlet No. 19*

BIBLIOGRAPHY

(1958) *Secondary Education for all. A New Drive.* (*White Paper*)

Central Advisory Council for Education (England) (From 1944)
(1954) *Early Leaving*
(1959) *Fifteen to Eighteen* (Crowther Report)
(1963) *Half our Future* (Newsom Report)
(1967) *Children and their Primary Schools* (Plowden Report)

Advisory Council on Education in Scotland
(1947) *Secondary Education*

Central Advisory Council for Education (Wales)
(1949) *The Future of Secondary Education in Wales*

Department of Education and Science (From 1964)
(1965) 'The Organisation of Secondary Education'. Circular 10/65. July
(1966) 'School Building Programmes'. Circular 10/66. March

Committee on Higher Education
(1963) *Higher Education* (Robbins Report)

University of Oxford
(1966) *Report of Commission of Inquiry* (Franks report)

Books, Pamphlets and Journals

ALLSOP, E., & GRUGEON, D. (1966) *Direct Grant Grammar Schools*, Fabian Society.
A.M.A., The, journal of the Incorporated Association of Assistant Masters.
ASSISTANT MASTERS ASSOCIATION (1958) *Comprehensive Secondary Education.* (1967) *Teaching in Comprehensive Schools, a second report.*
BANKS, OLIVE (1955) *Parity and Prestige in Secondary Education*, Routledge & Kegan Paul.
BANTOCK, G. H. (1954) *Freedom and Authority in Education*, Faber.
BENN, C. *Comprehensive Reorganisation Surveys*, 1966-7 to 1972.
BENN, C., and SIMON, B. (1970) *Half Way There*, McGraw Hill, 2nd ed. 1972, Penguin Education.
BERG, LEILA (1968) *Death of a Comprehensive*, Penguin.
BISHOP, T. J. H., and WILKINSON, R. (1967) *Winchester and the Public School Elite*, Faber.
BROWN, S. C., *et al* (1957) 'The Common English Syllabus in the Comprehensive School', in B. Simon (ed.), *New Trends in English Education*, MacGibbon & Kee.
BURT, (SIR) CYRIL, (ed.) (1934) *How the Mind Works*, Allen & Unwin.

BIBLIOGRAPHY

BURT, (SIR) CYRIL (1943) 'The Education of the Young Adolescent: the Psychological Implications of the Norwood Report', *British Journal of Educational Psychology*, November 1943.

BURT, (SIR) CYRIL (1959) 'The Examination at Eleven Plus', *British Journal of Educational Studies*, May 1959.

CAMPBELL, F. (1956) *Eleven Plus and All That*, Watts.

CARTER, N. W. (1967) 'Widening "Modern" Horizons', in B. Simon (ed.), *New Trends in English Education*, MacGibbon & Kee.

CLARKE, (SIR) FRED (1940) *Education and Social Change*, Sheldon Press.

COLE, M. (1953) *What is a Comprehensive School?* London Labour Party.

COX, C. B., and DYSON, A. E. (eds), *Black Paper 1* (1969), *Black Paper 2* (1969), *Black Paper 3* (1970).

CURTIS, S. J. (1952) *Education in Britain since 1900*, Dakers.

DAVIS, J. A. M. (1962) 'Examinations in Secondary Modern Schools', *Forum*, Vol. 4, No. 2.

DENT, H. C. (1942) *A New Order in English Literature*, University of London Press.

DENT, H. C. (1949) *Secondary Education for All*, Routledge & Kegan Paul.

DENT, H. C. (1952) *Change in English Education*, University of London Press.

DENT, H. C. (1954) *Growth in English Education, 1944-52*, Routledge & Kegan Paul.

DOUGLAS, J. W. D. (1964) *The Home and the School*, MacGibbon & Kee.

Education, weekly organ of the Association of Education Committees.

EGGLESTON, S. J. (1967) 'Some environmental correlates of extended secondary education in England'. *Comparative Education*, March 1967.

ELIOT, T. S. (1948) *Notes Towards the Definition of Culture*, Faber.

FIRTH, C. G. (1963) *Comprehensive Schools in Coventry and Elsewhere*, Coventry Education Committee.

FLOUD, J. (1961) 'Reserves of Ability', *Forum*, Vol. 3, No. 2.

FLOUD, J., and HALSEY, A. H. (1956) *Social Class and Educational Opportunity*, Heinemann.

FORD, B. (1965) 'The Ford Report'. *Bristol Evening Post*, 22 June 1965.

FORD, JULIENNE (1970) *Social Class and the Comprehensive School*, Routledge & Kegan Paul.

Forum, independent educational journal (three issues per annum).

FREELAND, GEORGE (1957) 'The Unstreamed Junior School', in B. Simon (ed.), *New Trends in Education*, MacGibbon & Kee.

BIBLIOGRAPHY

GLASS, DAVID (ed.) (1954) *Social Mobility in Britain*, Routledge & Kegan Paul.

GRIFFITHS, A. (1971) *Secondary School Reorganisation in England and Wales*, Routledge & Kegan Paul.

HALSEY, A. H. (ed.) (1961) *Ability and Educational Opportunity*, O.E.C.D.

HALSEY, A. H. and GARDNER, L. (1953) 'Selection for Secondary Education', *British Journal of Sociology*, March 1953.

HEIM, ALICE (1954) *The Appraisal of Intelligence*, Methuen.

HUGHES, H. D. (1955) *A Socialist Education Policy*, Fabian Society.

JAMES, ERIC (1949) *The Content of Education*, Harrap.

JAMES, ERIC (1951) *Education for Leadership*, Harrap.

Journal of Education, independent educational journal (monthly). Ceased publication in 1958.

KANDEL, I. L. (1955) *The New Era in Education*, Harrap.

KING, H. R. (1962) 'Comprehensive School—a Pattern of Achievement', *Forum*, Vol. 5, No. 1.

KOGAN, M. (ed.) (1971) *The Politics of Education*, Penguin.

LABOUR PARTY (1942) *Annual Conference Report*.

LABOUR PARTY (1950) *Annual Conference Report*.

LABOUR PARTY AND T.U.C. (1926) *From Nursery School to University*.

L.C.C. (LONDON COUNTY COUNCIL) (1947) *London School Plan*.

L.C.C. (LONDON COUNTY COUNCIL) (1953) *The Organisation of Comprehensive Secondary Schools*.

L.C.C. (LONDON COUNTY COUNCIL) (1961) *London Comprehensive Schools; a survey of sixteen schools*.

LOVETT, WILLIAM (1841) *Chartism*.

MARSDEN, D. (1971) *Politicians, Comprehensives and Equality*, Fabian Society, Tract 411.

MASON, S. C. (1957) *The Leicester Experiment*. Councils and Education Press. (New editions entitled *The Leicester Experiment and Plan*, in 1960, 1963, 1964.)

NATIONAL ASSOCIATION OF LABOUR TEACHERS (1929) *Education, a Policy*, C.W.S.

NATIONAL ASSOCIATION OF SCHOOLMASTERS (1964) *The Comprehensive School*.

NATIONAL FOUNDATION FOR EDUCATIONAL RESEARCH (1964) *Local Authority Practices in the Allocation of Pupils to Secondary Schools*.

NATIONAL FOUNDATION FOR EDUCATIONAL RESEARCH (1968) *Comprehensive Education in England and Wales*.

NATIONAL FOUNDATION FOR EDUCATIONAL RESEARCH (1970) *Comprehensive Education in Action*.

NATIONAL FOUNDATION FOR EDUCATIONAL RESEARCH (1972) *A Critical Appraisal of Comprehensive Education*.

NATIONAL UNION OF TEACHERS (1928) *The Hadow Report and After*.

NATIONAL UNION OF TEACHERS (1935) 'Memorandum of evidence submitted to the Consultative Committee of the Board of Education'.

NATIONAL UNION OF TEACHERS (1964) *The Reorganisation of Secondary Education*.

PARKINSON, M. (1970) *The Labour Party and the Organization of Secondary Education, 1918-65*, Routledge & Kegan Paul.

PEDLEY, ROBIN, AND OTHERS (1954) *Comprehensive Schools Today*, Councils and Education Press.

PEDLEY, ROBIN (1956) *Comprehensive Education, A New Approach*, Gollancz.

PEDLEY, ROBIN (1963) *The Comprehensive School*, Penguin, 3rd ed. 1969.

RÉE, H. (1956) *The Essential Grammar School*, Harrap.

ROWE, A. W. (1967) 'I abolished Streaming', *New Education*, April.

Schoolmaster, The, organ of the National Union of Teachers; title changed to *The Teacher* in 1963.

RUBINSTEIN, D., AND STONEMAN, C. (1970) *Education for Democracy*, Penguin Education; 2nd ed. 1972.

SIMON, BRIAN (1953) *Intelligence Testing and the Comprehensive School*, Lawrence & Wishart.

SIMON, BRIAN (1955) *The Common Secondary School*, Lawrence & Wishart.

SIMON, BRIAN (ed.) (1957) *New Trends in Education*, MacGibbon & Kee.

SIMON, BRIAN (1965) *Education and the Labour Movement, 1870-1920*, Lawrence & Wishart.

SIMON, BRIAN (1971) *Intelligence, Psychology and Education*, Lawrence & Wishart.

SIMON, SHENA (LADY) (1948) *Three Schools or One*, Muller.

SMITH, J. E. (1958) 'A Comprehensive School organised in age groups', *Inside the Comprehensive School*, N.U.T.

T.E.S. *Times Educational Supplement*, (weekly).

TAWNEY, R. H. (1922) *Secondary Education for All*, Allen & Unwin.

TAYLOR, WILLIAM (1963) *The Secondary Modern School*, Faber.

THOMPSON, D. (1965) 'Towards an Unstreamed Comprehensive School', *Forum*, Vol. 7, No. 3.

THOMSON, GODFREY (1929) *A Modern Philosophy of Education*, Allen & Unwin.

TRADES UNION CONGRESS (1939) Statement on the Spens Report.

TRADES UNION CONGRESS (1942) Memorandum on Education after the War.

Trends in Education (1967) 'Community School', April 1967. Quarterly published by the Department of Education and Science.

VERNON, P. E. (ed.) (1957) *Secondary School Selection*, Methuen.

BIBLIOGRAPHY

WEBB, SIDNEY (1908) 'Secondary Education', in H. B. Binns, *A Century of Education, 1808-1908*, Dent.

YATES, A. and PIDGEON, D. A. (1957) *Admission to Grammar Schools*, Newnes.

YOUNG, M. (1961) *The Rise of the Meritocracy*, Thames & Hudson.